OUT OF ORDER

Rob Donnelly

Create the Day Publications

Copyright © 2019 by Robert Donnelly

All rights reserved. No part of this publication may be reproduced, distributed or transmitted in any form or by any means, without prior written permission.

Create the Day Publications
Canberra ACT, Australia
Book Layout © 2016 BookDesignTemplates.com
Cover designed by Emilie van Os-Schmitt
Out of Order/ Rob Donnelly. -- 1st ed.
ISBN 978-0-6485822-1-2

To my strong and loving Liz

To Nick who goes from strength to strength

And the boys whose lives ended too early.

DISCLAIMER

I have recreated events and conversations from my memories of them. I have changed the names of individuals to maintain their anonymity.

FOREWORD

I wrote this book and now I have a dilemma. I have expressed, as clearly as memory allows, my experience of the men I lived with during my monastic life in the 1990s. There are a couple of times when I mention a particular priest who positively inspired me. He is known in the book by his initials JV. I saw him as a man so steeped in the spirituality of the Carmelite Order that he was luminous with the joy and promise found in it. I saw him as embodying the best that a life dedicated to prayer and spiritual reflection could achieve.

I found out, after completing my book, that there was another side to JV. He was a priest who used the language and ideas of spirituality to manipulate and sexually abuse a woman. He continued this abhorrent behaviour through to the end of his life.

This revelation has left me wondering what I should do with my memory of the man. This is my dilemma. Should I surgically remove all positive reference to him? If I did, then the account of my own experience would be incomplete. Should I counter every positive statement about him with a hefty reminder of the hidden side of his life? I'm not sure that would work either. I suspect the most powerful thing to do is to present the man as I experienced him and trust that you will remember this other dark reality of his life – and if you are moved to outrage or grief, then I assure you, you are not alone.

maybe there
maybe not
I talk to you
regardless

PART ONE

CHAPTER ONE

I was Jonah in the belly of the whale for the last six months of 1999. I was thirty-two years old and had walked away from everything that was my life and identity. Convulsive forces were breaking me apart. I was thrown about by rage and pain and the electric strike of memories, the jarring sound of others' judgements, the absence of friends, and the distance from my family that was measured by my shame.

Some days I sobbed until I was empty, curled like an embryo, lost in that dark place. My head pounded. My body ached. I stared at the brick wall beside my bed, with nothing in my head until another memory sent me spiralling down again.

I had become somebody. Now I was unravelling into nobody again. Once knit together. Now picked apart. Bare bones. Bare man. Annihilation full steam ahead. I called for you, but you were long gone. Maybe you were never there at all.

I walked when I found energy. I went up to Centennial Park and took the long circuit, under the canopy of trees, and almost convinced myself that I was an ordinary person. If I walked fast enough, I could leave the sadness behind and lose myself in the crowd of eastern suburbs joggers, dog walkers, frenetic cyclists and women debriefing with exercise companions about the impossible people in their lives. I looked around at all that perfectly attired, casual normality and I felt like a refugee. I was from a country such people could never understand.

I walked down to Clovelly Beach when winter dissolved into spring. I took the coastal track through the graveyard down to Bronte, where leather-skinned oldies congregated, and over the headland to the long stretch of Bondi. The waves rolled through me as I watched them. I could taste the salt that settled on my lips and feel the sun on my skin. All the elements rubbed hope into my flesh and blood.

Some nights I filled my ears with music, turned myself into a whirling dervish, chanted songs as I once chanted psalms, and gloried in the force that was unravelling me. I then felt nothing but the strength and honesty of my beautiful failure, my *felix culpa*, my lucky fault. It was there in the cells of my body, the ache of my sex, the beat of my heart, the dark reaching strength of my appetites. It was there in the spin of my senses: a kaleidoscopic chorus of sensations asserting life.

I was staying in an apartment underneath an aged-care facility where old priests were drifting into their twilight years and the enveloping fog of dementia. It wasn't where I wanted to be, but I had little money and I didn't fancy sleeping rough in Sydney.

I had certain things in common with those old men above me. I had been prostrate in a church, as they had once been, while angels and saints had been invoked. I had felt the hands of a bishop on my head and the holy oils pressed into my hands. I had said masses, heard confessions and carried out baptisms and funerals.

Some people still considered me a priest. They no

doubt prayed that I would get over whatever I was going through and go back to the monastery and the ministry and the work in spirituality and the popular business of retreats. They prayed for me at a safe distance from the leprous complication of my life and waited for something that was never going to happen. They hoped the grace of ordination would bring me back from the abyss. It didn't. The abyss claimed me more fully than the priesthood and the monastery ever could. Truth was in the abyss. Truth was in the gravity of falling. If you taught me one thing it was this: there is no grace purer than gravity.

CHAPTER TWO

I walked across the fields to Bondi Junction and caught the train to North Sydney once a week. I've always liked trains. I like the mesmerising sound and sway and the anonymity of the subterranean crowds. I like the heat of jostling bodies and the way that busy spaces like Town Hall Station are grazed with memories. The journey to North Sydney gave me time to be mindless as I moved from the tunnels into the flickering shadows of the bridge. It was a time of welcome emptiness before I sat in a room, opposite my psychologist, and tried to find words to speak about where I had come from and what I was going through.

Her office was tucked behind the shrine to Australia's first saint. I pressed a sequence of touchpad numbers and entered a discrete door at the rear of the building. Her office was bright with morning light. There was a desk in one corner covered with a stack of papers and files. Signs of a busy work life. A low table and comfortable chairs were nearer the door. She lit a candle on the table before the session began. It flickered tentatively and wove a short thread of smoke in the air. I watched the flame as she settled in the chair opposite me.

She was an older woman – a nun psychologist – a gentle, grey pragmatist in the overlapping worlds of religion and psychology. She knew the dramas of religious life. She knew the bright dark realities of the church. She had worked with all manner of broken people: abused and abusers, addicts, neurotics, psychotics, strugglers and battlers. Now she worked with me.

She looked at me with the soft robust disposition that certain nuns inhabit. Her attention drew me from the belly of the beast if only for one hour a week. For that hour, she was a witness to my words, my sobbing and shame, and all the accrued frustration of my life. For an hour I felt the shivering essence of my newborn state cradled in the eyes of this woman.

"Where are you today?"

Every session began with this question of geography. Not how are you or why are you, but where are you. My life was spreading out in a growing map of stories, fracture lines, fragmented memories, string patterns of causal speculation. I could be anywhere in that tentative landscape, at any moment of the day or night, so the nun's question was always relevant. Where are you today? Name the starting point. The rest will follow. Tracks around the mystery of life. Each word a step. Each meeting a song.

And now it's time to begin again.

Can you see the boy I once was? Five foot ten, a mop of ungainly sandy hair half covering my eyes, a troubling cluster of pimples on my chin, clad in a T-shirt, jeans and a dirty pair of sneakers. It was July 1986. A cold Hobart morning spread across the valley in partial light and frost and river mist.

It was my nineteenth birthday. I was with three mates in a near empty campus bar. We were all Christian Brother old boys, imprinted with the leash that had been around our necks for the duration of our adolescence. We were smart enough to go to university, dumb enough to do what was expected, clueless about freedom and intoxicated by it. We were the last students to know the joy of wasting time on campus, without incurring a lifetime's debt. The baby-boomer dream of a better world was over. We were the ones to tread water in their wake – gormless, distracted, gen X through and through.

Bobbie was the cool guy in the gathering. He knew when bands had sold out and gone commercial six months before anyone else. He voiced his views with a cocky self-assurance, combined with curly-haired Italian charm, a quick flash of a smile, and a flourish of cosmopolitan sophistication. Simon was lost in the academic world. His disillusionment had a sharp edge that came out after a few beers. He was the first to drop out and get an honest job. Clown was freckle-faced and unpredictable, joking one minute and moody the next. His nickname didn't do him justice. There was more going on in him than he let on.

I was sitting at the table with them and staring at the floor, as though truth might be deciphered in the beer-stained carpet. That was me. Mostly full of daydreams. Barely present at all. Adrift on an unnamed spectrum. I looked up, awakened from my dreaming world, refocused on the outside world of people and conversations. The challenging world where I never quite believed I could hold my own. But I tried anyway, because I was meant to be a man now. I affected an unconvincing casual air, the way I imagined one of the boys might do. I laughed at a joke. I responded to a ribbing. I played the part of an old schoolmate alongside three others.

A video game was pinging beside the toilet doors, inviting any comers to enter a pixilated wrestling tournament. A replay of a South Australian football game was on the television that hung from the ceiling. Clean glasses rattled as they were racked up for another day's business. It was too early for drinking. The post-lecture surge would come later. We were mooching around wondering about the day ahead.

Clown decided to drive us up the mountain. His car was a clapped-out beast. It coughed smoke through South Hobart and Cascades, then chugged up the long ascent of Pinnacle Road until we came to a locked gate halfway up. The conditions ahead were unsafe for driving. We clambered out of the car and into the hard world of snow and ice. There were clouds all around, playing shadow games with the sun, and a buffeting southerly wind threw punches as we staggered on the ice. We launched into an indiscriminate battle fought with balls of gravelly snow. They splattered and stung our bodies as we yelped with feigned fury. Dirty, white balls arched through the air. Some disintegrated before they hit a target. We ran and charged at each other, skidding on the ice, breathless, cold and laughing.

My fingers froze and my knuckles turned blue. I launched a ball at no-one in particular, then realised, too late, that the others had already jumped in the car. They yelled happy birthday out the window, as Clown pulled a U-turn and headed down the mountain road. I stood shivering, halfway up Mount Wellington, wearing nothing but a dirty, wet T-shirt and jeans.

I waited and told myself they'd be back. They were dickheads, but they weren't total bastards. They knew hypothermia was a joke gone too far. It wasn't long before I heard them return. They played silly buggers for a while, stopping so I almost reached the car and then pulling away a further distance. I kept my cool in the freezing cold. They eventually relented and let me in.

Simon had wisely arrived at the view that we needed to find a pub. It was my birthday after all. We went to the Fern Tree Tavern and were greeted by the sweet smell of burning slabs of eucalyptus in the fireplace. We ordered jugs of beer and took over a pool table beside a window. Beer and pool had become the foundation of our first year of adult life and university existence.

There was something perfect about that moment: the chatter of mates, the vigorous chalking of a pool cue, the sound of balls racked up and struck, the staccato rhythm of a race call on the radio by the bar, the crackling radiance of the fire and its slow, fingering warmth pressing life back into my body. It was my first experience of adult contentment. I smiled as I looked out the window and saw snow drifting to the ground. I had grown up in the shadow of the mountain, but I had never experienced being in the middle of falling snow. Each flake descended with a gentle rocking motion as though winter had all the time in the world to turn the landscape white. It was one of the gentlest sights I'd ever seen. I drifted into a state of reverie, intoxicated by snow and steadily imbibed beer, feeling barriers dissolve inside me, everything easy, softened, careless. It wasn't long before words started sliding off my tongue like treacle, and my limbs were troubled by a world spinning on an increasingly precarious axis.

I was given a lift, that night, across the river to my home. My head was already throbbing with the aftereffects of the day's festivities. I was sober enough to know my body's drunken treachery. My tongue was still thick and uncooperative. My legs were inclined to weave in knots, rather than compel me in a straight line.

I knew there was going to be disappointment on the other side of the front door, as I clambered around trying to marry the key to the lock. I could see the kitchen light spilling into the hall. My tiny mother was standing there, wearing one of her waterproof aprons, ready to hug me and sing me happy birthday. Her delight died on her face when she saw me. There was sadness in her eyes, a sigh of disappointment, a shake of the head, a too familiar choreography of despair. She thought I might be different – her good, youngest boy, her baby – but now I was just another male with a taste for the grog, a Trojan Horse of unpredictable conflict, another staggering presence to worry about through the long hours of the night.

She sat down in the lounge room and I sat at her feet. I tried to reassure her that I had only had a few drinks and that I was still her good boy. There was no repairing the damage. There was only disappointment. She went to bed heartbroken. I went to bed with a throbbing head, spinning in a centrifuge of guilt, forming a fevered resolution that I would never cause her such pain again, and I would do whatever it took to set things right in the universe. I would make good in some way, even if I had to sever all my connections to make it possible.

CHAPTER THREE

It was another winter, but a solitary one. I started avoiding people after my nineteenth birthday. It was easy. I had always been a loner deep down. I often struggled with the demands of sociability. There was a certain relief in giving up.

I walked to the bus stop three houses along from my home. The grass was crisp under foot, and my breath was cloudy in the air. I could see the mountain over the rooftops and across the river. The clouds had parted and the mountain was crowned with snow.

I always arrived at the bus stop before the girl who lived across the road from me. She was a college student and the daughter of a religious minister. That was the extent of my knowledge about her. I knew the day would be good when she came out her front door and walked up to the bus stop. The time between the thump of her door and her arrival was the highlight of my day.

I had made the mistake of not saying hallo to her on the first morning we caught the bus together. If I had managed it that first time, then it would have been an established habit. But I didn't say a word on that first morning, and my confidence was silently shredded every morning after that. Even the thought of saying hallo caused my heart to race too fast.

I imagined if I spoke it would come out as some strangulated noise, the whine or whimper of some creature less than a man, and then there would be nothing to do but scurry away in embarrassment and shame. And so, we stood silently waiting for the bus at a distance. I barely dared to glance at her, though I couldn't help notice when a breeze stirred through her unbound, long hair. She sometimes punctuated the waiting with a sigh. I thought her sighs might be significant, but I had no idea how to interpret them and I didn't have the courage to ask.

My heart returned to its regular rhythm once I accepted that this was simply another morning of silent failure. The bus arrived. Its doors flew open. She got on, then I followed and sat some distance away. The bus travelled downhill to the main road, pushed through the suburbs, went around Kangaroo Bay, over the hill beside the shopping centre, over the long arch of the bridge that spanned the river, and then sped along the western shore of the river and into the city.

I sat and stared out the window. I was relieved that the tension of the bus stop was over for another day, but worried by the chokehold that silence had on me. What was I good for if I couldn't even manage to say hallo to a girl I saw every morning?

I got off the bus at the city centre and started walking. I was made right through the physical rhythm, so I walked, rather than catching another bus, from the city to the campus. I walked along the streets of Battery Point and felt open to the elements: the buffeting force of a southerly breeze; the sunlit glimmer of the waters off Sandy Bay; the drama of clouds curling, merging and breaking across the broad expanse of the river valley. My final consolation, as I walked the stretch of shoreline leading to the campus, was the whir and whistle of yacht masts along the waterfront.

The leaden feeling, as I looked ahead and saw the university, put me hand in hand with my eleven-year-old schoolboy self. In the later years of primary school, under the dark reign of a malevolent baby-boomer principal, I took increasingly elaborate journeys when walking from the city bus stop up the hill to the squat, brick school where I was doing time. The most direct route was about one kilometre. I stretched my journey to double and even triple the distance. Between the age of ten and twelve, I'd walk up Liverpool Street, and the steep incline of Molle Street, and around the back hills of West Hobart. There was freedom and adventure for as long as my feet were making distance and going anywhere but school. I imagined Hobart was the shimmering surface of a mythical landscape that I bravely traversed every morning.

I sometimes had a companion in my walking adventures. His name was David. He had a mop of blond hair and was among my oldest friends. I had known him since I was five. He was smart but quirky. He seemed to understand and share the inclination to venture up unknown streets, find new routes and explore unknown territories.

One day, in grade five, we attended an athletic carnival on the Hobart Domain. I was with David and his younger brother after the carnival finished. We decided to find a different way to get down the hill to the bus. We cut through a block of land and were suddenly confronted by an angry Greek at the lower end of the property.

"What are you kids doing?" he yelled. "You're up to no good."

He glared at us with bewildering anger. His face was tomato red and great throbbing veins popped out the side of his neck. It was as though we had unwittingly stumbled into the territory of some angry Mediterranean god. We ran back up the hill fuelled by fear but also outrage at being told off for no obvious reason. There was an orange on the ground. David's brother picked it up.

"We ought to throw it at the crazy bastard," I said.

Before another word was uttered the orange was flying through the sky in a great arc. It was a moment of magnificent rebellion.

The next morning the thing I dreaded most in all the world happened. We were called up to the principal. We ascended the creaky wooden stairs and entered the dark of the grade-six classroom. The principal loomed over us like a wild, bearded ogre. He looked us up and down. He could smell the fear. He bristled with the pleasure of it. A smirk crept over his lips.

"I received a complaint from a member of the public yesterday afternoon," he said. "Three boys from the school were not only trespassing on private property but also threw an orange at him. I already know it was the three of you. I'll talk to you individually."

I disintegrated in tears when I faced him alone.

Profuse apologies tumbled out of my mouth. I was raw with fear and suddenly realised how little courage I had. It was a terrible moment of self-recognition. I was nothing like the movie heroes I loved. They might have been prisoners of war, victims of torture, exhausted and wounded soldiers on some frontline or sleep-deprived spies bound and interrogated, but they always stood up to the menace in front of them. They looked their enemies in the eye with their chins raised high. They answered abuse with a smart retort and a defiant stare. Each and every one of them was an unconquerable man.

I couldn't find the faintest skerrick of their kind of courage in myself. All I had was snot and tears, tremulous fear and panic, a clamouring desperation to appease the bastard ogre with thunder in his eyes and malicious pleasure in the turn of his lips. I realised I was prepared to curl up in complete submission to avoid the pain of the place of punishment commonly referred to as the Crying Room. I was nothing but a coward.

"What's it going to be," said the principal. "The Crying Room or after school detention?"

David was a pragmatist. He wanted the speed of six quick cracks of leather on a proffered hand.

"Let's just get it over with," he said.

Fear paralysed me. The imagined pain had taken on a murderous magnitude. I said I'd rather it was detention, so that's how we ended up being punished. We wrote lines for two hours after school.

"Where will we walk next?" David asked, as we stood together on the school basketball court at recess the next day.

"Yeah, I don't know," I said. The feeling of dread still reverberated in me. Things could come undone so easily and, once undone, catastrophe was sure to follow.

"Might give it a miss for a while."

"But why?" he protested. "Why should what happened make a difference?"

"I don't know."

"But we're still mates?" he asked.

I shrugged and, with that mute gesture, I snuffed out the friendship. I could see he was sad. His head went down, and his shoulders slumped as he walked away. It wasn't that I blamed David for the situation. A great deal of the fault was on my shoulders. It just seemed safer for me to walk alone. I stood on the basketball court, in my fortress of solitude, safe from further social complication, little knowing I had started carving a behavioural groove that would last decades of my life.

It was years later. I was still walking alone along elaborate routes. The university campus loomed ahead, and there was the familiar feeling of dread: going where I didn't want to go, doing what I didn't want to do, soaking in the final moments of a vivid and alive world, before entering the sterile linoleum world of the engineering building.

I had wanted to be a writer since I was eight years old. Yet there I was learning the mathematical fine points of a strategic warfare to master nature and make it submit, to push on with development, to make things bigger and better – concrete poured into form-work, dams raised to hold back wild rivers, all the wonder of the universe turned into cog-like, utilitarian components. It jarred against everything inside me and was totally foreign to the way I read my world. But there was nothing new in that jarring experience. I had felt it since I started school. It just showed I had to squeeze harder to fit into the world and all its expectations.

CHAPTER FOUR

I went to the university refectory before my first morning class. I bought a newspaper beforehand and stood in the middle of the large dining room, watching the vending machine drop a cup in place, then dispense my coffee. It was always watery with a shot of unconvincing milk, but the fact that it was unsatisfactory didn't matter. It was part of my routine along with the morning walk and reading the newspaper. I needed routine. I needed ritual. It expressed some primitive instinct inside me: do these things and you will get through today unscathed.

I was interested in politics and world events. Hawke was prime minister of Australia. Reagan was president of the United States. Gorbachev was in power in the USSR. The Cold War was a reality and Berlin was still divided by the wall. There were hints of change, but nothing substantial was happening. My fingertips turned black with print ink as I worked my way across the broadsheet pages. I sipped my coffee then drifted into a half-dazed state. Nothing in the paper really mattered.

There weren't many people in the refectory at first. A few drifted in and settled together at a table on the far side of the room. The air was soon filled with an impassioned argument. A battle of the sexes about something. One serious male voice rose to hammer home some point of monumental importance. Then a comic in the group cracked the tension with an observation that conjured an eruption of laughter. A girl threw her arm around the serious boy's shoulders, playfully swaying him back and forth, then she whispered something in his ear, and he laughed.

I looked up from my paper and across at their free-flowing world and wondered where they found their ease and confidence. I didn't have a skerrick of it. I couldn't even manage to say hallo to the girl who lived across the road from me. Yet there they were, the same age as me, with their precocious intellects and languid, entangling limbs, lips pressed to ears, hormones near combustion.

Their world seemed impossible to me. My virgin body, bound with suspicions of inadequacy, was a tight clenched thing in comparison. I sat at the table, with my watery coffee and newspaper, absorbing everything that happened across the room: every inflection in a voice, every wave of laughter, the free-flowing torrents of a life that was beyond me. I dropped my eyes when anyone looked in my direction. I couldn't bear the thought of becoming an object of their laughter.

I walked to the bottom of the campus where the engineering building sat beside chemistry and law. I had gone from an all-boys Christian Brothers' school to the male-dominated world of engineering. There was abundant testosterone in the faculty, and a professionally bound boyish passion for crushing and blowing objects up and winning the annual university chariot race where billycarts raced through the campus in pursuit of honour, glory and a keg of beer.

I could count the number of girls studying in the faculty on one hand. There was a mysterious Iranian woman who I had shared a few classes with in my first year. She was always accompanied by a man. I presumed he was her husband. I sometimes daydreamed in lectures, imagining he had a scimitar close at hand, to slice any infidel who might look at his wife the wrong way. There was a tall girl, with tight-curled hair, who was a year ahead of me. She seemed to hold her own, in that predominantly male world, far more successfully than I did.

I sat in classes through the morning, taking down the scribbled symbolic lines that had something to do with energy transference, the concentration and dissipation of compressive and tensile stress, the amplitude of waves and the relentless pull of gravity. It was an induction into the number-crunching mysteries that resulted in skyscrapers rising to the clouds without toppling and dams holding back deep-pressured volumes of water without failing.

I spent my afternoons in laboratories carrying out experiments. My thermodynamics lecturer was a portly man with a walrus moustache and an old-world charm. He was the type to own a fob watch and smoke a pipe. All of that was apt as his specialty made him master of a steam-punk laboratory where fire met water, pistons pounded and endless gauges measured mysterious things. I was like a deer in the headlights in all the laboratories, but the explosive potential of the thermodynamics lab was the most frightening of all.

We had been allocated lab partners at the beginning of the semester. I found myself working with two Indonesian students. They rarely spoke English, so I was the odd man out. One afternoon we were faced with the task of working with a great steam-powered beast. It was like a train engine bolted to the floor, and it towered above us.

My partners walked off in the middle of the exercise. They picked up their nearby prayer mats and disappeared to face Mecca and pray. Afterwards they shot the breeze over a casual post-prayer cigarette. I was left alone with the beast. I desperately raced around reading gauges and recording information. I hoped my own busy devotion might keep the thing placated. I swear I could hear the strain of the rivets from the pressure of all that hemmed in power. There was entropy at play somewhere in the bowels of it: an increasing amount of energy that wouldn't submit, that wouldn't be rendered useful, that wouldn't lead to anything but increasing disorder. Just the thought of that made me nervous.

At the end of that anxious afternoon, the lab session arrived at the same result as every other session I had endured. Laboratory measurements were a spray of gunfire from a whirling, blindfolded shooter compared to the elegant smooth curve of theory. Random reality proved theory a lie and I knew if I was looking for the truth, whatever that truth might be, I was never going to find it in engineering.

CHAPTER FIVE

It was night and the house was still. I was awake, but that wasn't unusual – I had wrestled with insomnia since I was a child. I got out of bed and crept down the hall, carefully avoiding the creaking floorboards that always woke my mother up. My foot landed on an unchartered board. It squeaked. Mum stirred in the dark of her room.

"Are you alright?" she murmured.

"Yes," I replied, regretting that my nocturnal solitude had been broken.

I went into the kitchen, closed the door behind me, and poured a glass of milk. I went and collected my notebook and pen from the lounge room, then sat on the kitchen bench beside the radio. The announcer murmured a love-song dedication message before playing Whitney Houston. I turned the radio down as she started the build up to her bellowing chorus of sincerity. I drank a mouthful of milk, then took up my pen and notepad and started fishing for words.

I imagined I was walking. I spent half my days walking so it was easy to imagine. But where was I walking? I hunted around for the right setting. I thought of my favourite sci-fi movie, *Bladerunner*, with its gritty streets and towering edifices of constantly changing neon. The feeling of foreboding seemed right, but the visual imagery didn't work. Where was I walking? Somewhere empty. I was walking alone. What a surprise. I was walking alone in a strangely twisted landscape. Something like a Dali painting. That was it. A landscape cracked like eggshells. Hollow underfoot. Buildings were twisted. Order had broken down. The neat marshalling lines of an engineered world had turned to dust. Alleluia.

I was walking through this landscape but where was I going? Why was I there? Who was I looking for in such a strange place? I was looking for my brothers. I somehow knew they were there. I was calling out, and my voice was echoing in strange, distorted ways across the landscape. Would I find them? Would they hear me? Would they recognise me?

My pen flew over the page of the notepad as I described my surreal journey. There was joy when I caught hold of a word, or even better a series of words, that rang true. Truth was there, flowing through my mind, racing in lines making words on a page. Truth was a scrawled thing, crossed out, reconfigured, puzzled over. A scribbled, evolving push into the unknown. Here was the thing that mattered. The sweet joyous something that mattered. An ability to create in the dark.

My real life began when I started finding words. Do you remember that moment? I paused and finished the milk. The Christian bikie, John Smith from the God Squad, came on the radio. He preached his message. He punctuated his words with occasional bursts of U2. They still hadn't found what they were looking for. His message was simple and direct. It seemed to carry the experience and struggles of ordinary life. I preferred his insights to the Sunday homilies of the priests in the church up the road. They rarely seemed to offer anything relevant to me.

I went into the lounge room and looked through

the venetian blinds. Pools of light punctuated the dark line of the street as it pushed up the hill. A cat darted across the front yard. Cicadas sounded from the dirt below the lawn. There was no breath of wind so the river, beyond the suburb, was close to a mirror surface. It reflected the back hills and mountains and the rim of suburban light along the western shore. But the deep business of the river kept on, despite that stillness. Its waters pushed out into Storm Bay and the Southern Ocean and the frozen world below.

I sat in a lounge chair facing my typewriter. It was as corpulent as a 1950s car. It was one of the few objects in my entire life that I truly loved. Its long, spindly keys tapped against the page like a chorus line. I loved the size and weight of it and relished the tap, smack, whir of word making that could make a world in the space of a single page. I set to work typing my journey poem, and when I finished I added it to the folder of poems that I had written on previous nights. The folder was filling with a patchwork testament that there was something inside me after all. I had thoughts and images and ideas. I had fire and passion. I had substance. I was somebody. I was real.

CHAPTER SIX

I wasn't used to the vulnerability of disclosure. It went against my lifelong instinct to stay safely hidden and below the radar. But my words were there, typed and bound together in a green lever-arch folder, silently demanding to be received by someone other than me. I handed the folder over to my parents. They took it away and read it over the course of the following day.

I felt raw with expectation when they came back, with my work, the next night. Mum looked slightly perplexed. She was no doubt concentrating on the delicate business of not putting her foot in it by saying the wrong thing.

"Now I know what you've been up to at night," she said. "It's very interesting," she added with a tentative nod.

"Yes. Certainly an interesting read," Dad said. His accompanying rattled sigh suggested he had more to say, but he thought better of it.

I smiled and said thanks and took the folder back. I'm not sure what I expected. Maybe some startling moment of recognition. *You have all of that in you! My boy, a literary genius, the world is surely your oyster now. You must write. Write my son. Write like there's no tomorrow. Forget this engineering nonsense. Forget any advice I gave you about writing being a nice hobby you could do on weekends. I must have been out of my mind to suggest such a thing. Pursue your destiny. Whatever it takes. You must. I insist.* Instead there was an awkward silence that seemed to transform my folder of poems into an outbreak of unexpected flatulence. It sat there, heavy in the air, and no-one knew if anything further needed to be said.

"Think I'll go to bed now," I announced as I took the folder and retreated to my bedroom. I could feel the presence of the chubby, bespectacled boy I once was.

They didn't get it, he grumbled. *How could they not get it? How could they not see it?*

I could feel his familiar frustration. His rally cry against a misunderstanding world. What could I say to him? People often don't get it. That illusive, mythical it. The it below the surface of words. The it that's always looking to be said, that's always waiting to be received. The it that's recognition and embrace, bond and undoing, tear fall and belonging. The it beneath the chorus of the world.

We're not going to give up are we? My boy-self spoke with the accrued wounded knowledge from all our previous defeats. *We can't just stop. There has to be someone who gets it.*

It would have been easy to give up. It would have made sense. But every night I found myself carefully walking through the hall, inadvertently causing floorboards to creak, assuring my mother that I was OK, and then sitting in the kitchen, drinking milk and writing poetry.

You know what came next. I had been circling you through all those poems and then, one night, I came up close and slipped inside you so deep I breathed the night air through your lungs. Gethsemane. We'll always have Gethsemane. There you were bowed down and sweating blood in the moonlit shadows of olive trees. Disciples asleep. The world asleep. You wide awake and staring at your impending death. Me wide awake and staring at my typewriter.

I hadn't felt the grip of that kind of biblical drama since I was a kid but there it was, inside me, looking for expression. I had avidly pursued multiple spiritual ideas since I started university. I haunted bookshops checking out every New Age book in stock. I had a passion for Jung. I dabbled in creative visualisation. I went through occasional bouts of meditating and chanting mantras. Yet there I was suddenly seized by what exactly? An unexpected bout of Christian piety? A flaming tongue? A touch of messianic delusion? You tell me.

How many times shall tomorrow pass? This night seems so short for dawn is near.

I thought I was Shakespeare rolling out those first lines. It was so impossibly easy. I was sure you were there, birthing those long stanzas, tremulous with the fear of death, stretched with the ingathering intent to make a kingdom.

I wrote until there was nothing left to write and then I read it over and again and again. My words. Your words. In me. In you. I read myself into you with a monastic instinct. I felt the words demanded to be read as they always do. There was no great charity in my desire to share what I wrote. I hoped the right reader might bring me some relief. Maybe I could pass you on and be done with it.

I tried to think of somebody who would understand the poem. It obviously had to be someone with a religious inclination otherwise they wouldn't understand. There was no-one appealing in the local suburban catholic landscape. Then I remembered I had a cousin who was a nun living in a strange monastic world behind bars. Her circumstances suggested the kind of radical madness that might recognise the madness of my poem and the crazy way I felt it alive inside me. I knew little of this nun cousin, other than that she regularly corresponded with Mum, but I settled on sending the poem to her.

CHAPTER SEVEN

My mother's niece lived in a catholic contemplative monastery in the hills above the northern city of Launceston. I met her once in my childhood. My family had been on holidays in the north. We were on our way home to Hobart when we drove to an unassuming place surrounded by bushland. Mum had mentioned that her niece was an enclosed nun. I had no idea what that meant until we entered a room with a perplexing row of iron bars along one wall. It reminded me of visiting a prisoner, but unlike a prisoner, my cousin was behind bars by choice.

Most of the conversation was between the adults in the room: my cousin and Mum and Dad. My brother Shane and I sat and offered a word here and there when a question or comment was directed our way. I looked through the bars, but there was nothing to see in her side of the room. It was plain walls and empty space, with no sign of the mysterious life that happened inside. I looked around for something of interest and saw a cupboard in the corner on our side of the bars.

"That's a turn," my cousin said. "You can open the door if you like."

I went over and opened the cupboard and looked in. There was a structure inside that was something like a wooden revolving door.

"It's how we pass things back and forth," she said with some enthusiasm. She laughed then suddenly spun the contraption around to reveal a holy card that she had sent from her side, to illustrate its usefulness. It was intriguing but strange and made me think of people with contagious diseases who had to be sealed up in isolation chambers.

I largely forgot about that perplexing visit to my cousin as I continued with the challenges of my 1970s childhood. Mum regularly exchanged letters with her. They came loaded with holy cards that the nuns printed, and there was usually a brief greeting at the bottom of the letter for my brother Shane and me. My cousin showed a particular interest in Shane's ongoing role as an altar server in the parish. She speculated, in one of her letters, that he might have the makings of a good priest. Her fishing expedition provoked a lot of laughter among us.

I settled on the view that my cousin was the right person to read my poem. It didn't occur to me to share it with the parish priest or one of the priests in the city. I had no sense of connection to any of them.

Was I making a distinction between the mysterious experience of connection that bubbled to the surface in my poetry, and the everyday priest-led business of the church? Maybe. Was it that I trusted women more than men? Quite probably. Was I drawn to my cousin because she was mysterious and otherworldly like some ancient Sybil in a cave, who would read the signs then erupt with a message from beyond? That might be overstating it, if we were talking about anyone else. I couldn't get excited about my future until I started imagining one with a deep unfolding sense of mystery and surrender.

I wrote a simple letter to her. I hoped she was well

and suggested she might find the enclosed poem of interest. I read the poem over again and wondered if she would understand. I folded the letter and poem and placed them in an envelope. I found the monastery address on old correspondence from her. I sealed the letter, affixed a stamp, and walked down to the letterbox at the corner shop. My heart was racing. I knew some kind of change would come from this moment. It was a strange sense of hope and dread, culminating in a vertiginous lurch in my intestines, as I pushed the letter through the slot, let go with my fingertips, and heard it fall into the dark. There was no retrieving it. There was no turning back. Gravity had taken hold. Whatever was coming was going to come and that's all there was to it.

I didn't say a word to my parents. I didn't say a word to anybody. I instinctively felt secrecy was a necessary element in the transaction. It was a hermetic seal that would hold the process in hiding and bring it to completion at the right moment. I really had read a lot of Jung. I waited and wondered what reply would come. I tried to get on with my life, but an anxious thread ran through the days. I checked the letterbox multiple times every afternoon. There were bills, junk mail, nothing more, disappointment.

Why was it taking so long? Didn't she like the poem? Did she take it as presumptuous or even blasphemous that I might write a poem in the voice of Christ? What would I do if there was no reply? What would it mean? I struggled as the days became a week and then longer and then, one afternoon, I arrived back from university.

"You have a letter from your Carmelite cousin," Mum said. She looked at me with intrigue but didn't say anything else.

I took the letter to my room and quickly opened it. Holy cards and prayer cards and tiny folded pieces of photocopied writing fell out of the envelope along with a letter. I quickly read the pages. "My dear Rob, it was such a welcome surprise to hear from you." And further on. "Your poem brought to mind one of our saints. I have enclosed some passages from his writing." I felt relief. Here was a substantial response to my poem, but it was more than that. There was a sense of recognition in it. The words I had hammered out on my typewriter late at night mattered beyond the imaginative drama of my own mind. My creation had a welcome place outside myself, a context, an arena of belonging. This nun cousin who I barely knew could see it. And now there were photocopied fragments of some great spiritual, poetic tradition spread over my bed.

CHAPTER EIGHT

My cousin's letter finished with an invitation to visit her in the monastery. This was no small thing. I didn't have a car and I had never been to Launceston on my own. I bought a bus ticket the following week, settled into a window seat, and watched as we made our way past Hobart's northern suburbs, crossed the river at Bridgewater, and travelled up the Midland Highway.

The bus motored through the Midlands towns: Pontville, Mangalore, Bagdad, Jericho and briefly stopped at Oatlands. The solitary nature of my journey seemed to cast these places in a new light. The familiar world was slipping past. The unknown loomed dead ahead. My head was buzzing with a sense of promise, gleaned from the literary samples my cousin had sent me, but I was dumbfounded about what to make of it in a practical sense.

The bus arrived in the middle of Launceston, and I got off with only a vague sense that the monastery was somewhere in the hills above the city. I got in a taxi.

"I want to go to the Carmelite monastery."

"Oh yeah, I know where that is," replied the driver.

He pulled out and started weaving through suburbs. I tried to make small talk though that's never been my strong point, and I was glad when we settled into an amicable silence. It didn't take long before we drove down a driveway to a pleasant-looking brick building. It had a fine spire above a wing that I presumed was the chapel. The striking impression of the monastery was one of uncluttered simplicity.

"Well, here we are," said the driver. I paid him and then convinced myself to get out of the car and get on with it.

I approached the front door, my heart hammering, and rang the bell. A pint-sized, brown-habited nun answered. She looked me up and down with a slight air of amusement, as though I was a peculiar little creature that had landed at her front door.

"You must be Rob," she said with a grin. "Well, come in. I will show you along to the parlour. Your cousin will be with you soon."

I waited in a room that was vaguely familiar from my childhood visit. It was so quiet I could hear the groan of every thought in my head. I tried to distract myself. I stared at the long row of bars. They were as perplexing now as when I was a kid. There was a cover, secured behind the bars, so it wasn't possible to look into the other side of the room. I heard unseen doors opening and closing and then a muffled greeting.

"Hallo Rob."

"Hallo," I replied to the voice behind the wall.

The barrier, behind the bars, opened and there she was. My cousin was a beaming pink face surfacing out of an ocean of brown and white fabric. She settled in a chair on the other side of the bars.

"You found your way," she said with a grin.

"Oh yes, the taxi driver knew where to go."

"I think most of them know us by now."

She started knitting and launched into conversation with little pause for breath. I could feel my eyes twist in knots as I tried to focus on her through the bars. I felt my vision slipping and sliding until my eyes started to ache with the effort. Her eyes were largely taken up with the knitting, but they occasionally shot up to look at me, when some significant thing was said about my prayer life or spirituality, and then they shot back down to the clattering business of her needles.

She explained that the nun I met at the front door had the role of an extern. She was allowed to be outside the enclosure, so she could deal with visitors and assorted other outside business. I asked about the practicalities of enclosure and heard there were times nuns had to go out to see medical specialists, for example, but otherwise the vocation was to live an enclosed life of prayer, from the time of entering the monastery through to death.

"Enclosure was at the heart of Our Holy Mother's vision of the contemplative life," she said.

"Do you mean Mary?"

"No. No, Rob. Our Holy Mother is Saint Teresa of Jesus or Teresa of Avila, as she's more commonly known. She is the founder of our order, the discalced reform. It might be good for you to read her *Life*. It's one of the books she wrote."

"I certainly like the photocopied pieces you sent me."

"Saint John of the Cross. Well, of course, he's a poet – one of the great poets of Spain. His work is studied and praised even by non-religious scholars. It isn't easy to understand for beginners, but the beauty of the writing is clear."

"I found it quite moving. The image of the flame."

"You did," eyes fully on me. "Well, that's good," eyes back to the knitting. "Of course, our saints, Teresa and John, are both Doctors of the Church. Their teaching is utterly reliable and true to the teaching of the church."

"I would like to read more of them."

"You should be able to buy copies of Saint John of the Cross's collected works and the first two volumes of Saint Teresa's works at the Catholic Bookshop in Hobart. The Kavanaugh Rodriguez translations. Good reading and prayer is the place to start. Of course, the two can work together. Our Holy Mother found this very helpful. *Lectio Divina* – divine reading – using what you read as an opening to prayer."

"I think I know what you mean," I said.

She listened to my meagre words with a downward-gazing intensity that could suck marrow from living bones. The conversation continued mostly as a nun-driven monologue. She spoke about family, my parents and our shared aunts and uncles, the practice of prayer, recent studies into the psychological benefits of prayer, papal encyclicals, the Second Vatican Council, the most recent reports in the Vatican newspaper *L'Osservatore Romano*, the trouble that possums were causing in the monastery garden, and a minutiae of facts concerning her much-loved Polish pope.

"Did you know he was quite an actor in his

youth?"

"No."

"Did you know he studied our Saint John of the Cross for his doctoral thesis, so Carmel has always been close to his heart?"

"No."

"Did you know he nearly died young when he was crossing the road, with his head elsewhere, and was nearly run over?"

"No."

She continued talking about the Pope with a familiarity that suggested he often dropped in for a cup of tea and a quick debrief about the details of his day. She sat, speaking, intensely listening, eyes darting, cheeks beaming, mouth smiling, knitting needles clicking clacking, fabric occasionally rustling, until the allocated visiting time was about to end. Finally, it was time to strike.

"Do you think you might be called to be a priest?"

I knew the question was coming, but it still blindsided me. It hung in the air for a moment. I looked through the bars at my cousin.

"I don't know," I whimpered.

She smiled and nodded. Closed the shutters on her side of the bars and was gone. It felt like the first act of a mystery play was over, and I wasn't comfortably in the audience but sitting in the middle of a stage with the spotlight focused on me. I came out of the parlour in a state of shell shock. My flustered state didn't seem surprising to the extern nun, as she showed me to the front door.

I had time before my bus departed from the city

down below. My head was full of noise and pressure, and I knew only the steadying rhythm of walking would help. There was nothing graceful about my first descent from a Carmelite monastery. I stumbled through the hillside suburbs of Launceston with my arms flailing from side to side, as I wondered what the hell was happening to me. It wasn't as though it was the first time I had been asked if I was meant to be a priest. It was an idea that had lingered on the periphery of my life since I was a boy.

I was forced to study Latin in my first year of high school. Geography was offered as an alternate subject the following year. My feelings were so strong I stood up, in the middle of the class, to argue my case for choosing geography. I had spent my childhood keeping my head down in classrooms, so this was a surprising act. It was all the more surprising because the teacher I faced was a crusty old Christian Brother who wielded a legendary thick leather strap specifically designed to keep pimply boys like me in line. He let me say my piece then advised me to sit. Nothing more was said on the matter.

The brother had an old-school approach to imparting catholicism. This was the last opportunity to drum the truths of faith into boys before the complete onset of hormones and the troubling ways of the modern world. He brought his strap down on the hands of boys who incorrectly answered questions regarding the God of love, his holy church, the holy sacraments, the unambiguously black-and-white realities of the moral life, and the eternal repercussions of sin. I succumbed to the pressure of his leather-wielding pedagogy. I imbibed and regurgitated it all and so won the religious knowledge prize at the end of the year.

The old brother made a point of visiting my home to deliver the prize and have a cup of tea with my mother.

"Yes, Mrs. Donnelly, young Robert has done well this year," he said then took a sip of tea.

"Regarding Latin, I think it's best that he continues with it. It may come in handy for his future."

I was sitting on a bus, a few years later, when I was still in high school. One of the older boys, a wiry, tough kid I knew from a safe distance, walked down from the back of the bus and eyed me. I dropped my eyes and hoped that might be enough to deflect any confrontation.

"Hey Donnelly!"

I looked up.

"What's your favourite scripture passage?"

"I don't have one," I replied.

"Rubbish. I know you've got one. Everyone knows you're the one who's going to be the priest."

The most disturbing thing was his apparent sincerity. He didn't seem to want to provoke any particular reaction. He wasn't looking for a fight. I would have been judged an easy beat. He didn't seem to particularly want to humiliate me, otherwise he would have pursued the matter until I cried or yelled or crumpled to the ground as a quivering mess. He clearly believed what he said, and he was happy to move on once he had asserted the truth of my destiny. I sat in a state of mute embarrassment for the rest of that bus ride home from school then, ten years later, I sat in a similar state on the bus ride home from Launceston to Hobart.

CHAPTER NINE

I went into the Hobart Catholic Bookshop and picked up copies of the collected works of Saint John of the Cross and the first two books of Saint Teresa of Avila's collected works. I found the Kavanaugh Rodriguez translations, just as my cousin instructed. While I struggled with the question of becoming a priest, with no sense of what that would even look like, I had no doubt there was power in these Carmelite books. I had felt it when I was reading the tiny, photocopied fragments of spiritual writing my cousin had sent in her first letter. And while her world with its iron bars and strict formalities was utterly foreign and bewildering to me, the deep current of life suggested in the spirituality I had sampled felt captivatingly true and hinted at the possibility of belonging.

The first time I read a passage of writing by a Carmelite mystic, it was like the moment in *The Wizard of Oz* when the black and white world is suddenly shot through with dazzling technicolour. I saw the world, the church and myself differently. My solitary inclinations were no longer a mere consequence of social ineptitude. They now had a holy meaning. They were sign of a nature that was inclined to the fierce gravity of divine intimacy. Your finger was applied directly to my heart, and if I felt shaken, it was the vigorous resonance of some kind of holy calling.

"You need to be careful with this one," the nun behind the counter at the bookshop warned as she picked up Saint John of the Cross and punched the price in the register. "It's quite intense and can be easily misunderstood."

I was taken aback. I would never have expected that the writing of any saint might come with a warning. I also felt a thrill that I was obtaining something with a kind of under-the-counter seriousness and potency. Something a little stronger than regular catholic punters could handle.

"It's OK," I replied, "I have a cousin in the Launceston Carmel."

I launched into Saint Teresa's *Life*. She came bustling out of the sixteenth century, with a self-deprecating flourish, as soon as I opened the book. She marshalled the details of her early life around opposing poles of virtue and vice, bemoaning the bad advice of poor-quality confessors, laying out the complicated threads of her own highly sociable personality, and emphasising the long years she had wasted being something less than authentic.

My eyes raced across the page, absorbing the first impact of this forty-something woman as she sat at her table, ink-dipped quill in hand, with the Inquisition present in every shadow. Big brother watched everything in its pursuit of religious purity. Purity was the ideal to be maintained and defended at all costs. Purity was everything: the purity of the faith, the purity of the soul – compliant and obedient, white as an altar cloth. It justified many acts of bastardry.

In the name of that purity, and pragmatic self-protection, neighbour reported neighbour. Family members reported their own flesh and blood. New Christians – the ones with Jewish blood, the families forced to convert – were particularly questionable. And women, always women, were in the firing line. They were judged prone to imaginative flights of fancy, hysteria and demonic possession.

Teresa lived in the midst of those hard, Inquisitorial times: an outspoken woman; the granddaughter of a Jewish converso; a teacher and writer – suspect in so many ways. She had set about reforming her religious order when the message of her surrounding world was all-pervasive. Keep your head down, be an unassuming woman, don't get carried away with yourself or the things that you experience. Make do with the tried-and-true customs, the safe behaviours, the vocal prayers and common pieties, the acceptable measures of being religious, the ways that have the imprimatur of men.

The woman who was writing captivated me; the older Teresa who was sitting in her new monastery. She was strong and assured. She dared to write and teach, and not only trust her experience of a deep call to quiet prayer but share it with others. This strong woman – the narrator with her determined determination – left me blind to the woman she had once been and the long unfree, inauthentic years that added up to decades where she submitted to that message of her world.

I failed to see this journey was the necessary prelude to real understanding: the journey through a compromised life, a stifled truth, the charade of appearances, and presumptions that others knew best by virtue of little more than their titles. It takes time for truths to emerge. It takes time for character to take full shape. It takes time for momentum to build. But I was young when I first met Teresa. I wasn't interested in the long arch of time or the gradual accrued benefit of long journeys. I wanted an end point I could seize and a resolution to my fringe-dwelling existence. I wanted something solid and certain, and I wanted it now.

CHAPTER TEN

I shared the dilemma of many people who were my age in Tasmania in the late 1980s. The future was stirring in our early-twenties' imaginations. The life we wanted, the life to come, was out there somewhere. A siren call laced through our dreams and half-constructed insights – the feeling of a potential needing to be realised, the restless twist and kick of possibility in desperate need of an opportunistic birth.

The future was out there: beyond the hills and mountains; beyond the waters; beyond the magnificent limit of the island world where we had grown up. It was out there, over there, somewhere on the mainland, and there was no getting around the fact that we had to leave the island to find it.

I shared that exile-bound dilemma, but my dream was a different creature from the ones that crept through most of my contemporaries' imaginations. There was nothing in me that was corporate bound. I couldn't imagine climbing a career ladder to a high-rise office, finding satisfaction in a fancy car and a splendid house, or measuring my self-worth according to the size of the budget that I managed. Engineering was an unconvincing step towards that world. I was still studying the degree, but the thought of building a life on it was nothing less than a horror to me.

The thing that I had, that I dreamed, and that was the cause of my sharing in the mainland bound dilemma was a sense of spiritual destiny. Teresa of

Avila was whispering in my ears. John of the Cross was stoking my poetic coals. And if religion is the opium of the people, then I was fast becoming a full-fledged addict. I read every spiritual book that I could lay my hands on. I injected ancient currents of spirituality into my veins and dreamed of better days ahead.

I was sitting in Hobart, but also in the hermitage of a monk named Thomas Merton in the 1960s, as I read his stories of fourth century men who fled into the desert to spend their lives praying, men whose sanctity was humility, whose self-awareness was of brokenness, whose outlook on others was compassionate. I read Merton's reflections on the human and humane connection that comes in authentic solitude and I wanted it. I wanted the deep dive within, the breaking open, and the compassionate connection to others. I wanted his hermitage with its smell of wood fire and its windows looking out at the changing seasons. I wanted elemental simplicity: silence and space to feel the gravity within, still and present in the river of time.

I read the English translation of an old Russian Orthodox book, *The Way of the Pilgrim*, that told the story of a man's journey across the barren Steppes, but that was also a journey into a state of unending prayer. I took the simple repetition of a Jesus-focused mantra to heart. I tried putting it into practice. Prayer married to breath and heartbeat: a steady repetition of love in flesh and blood.

I read and absorbed and felt increasingly compelled to find the place where I could realise my full spiritual destiny. It had to be the right place. It had to ring true with all this shaping flow that was running through me. There was nowhere in Tasmania; nowhere that my presumptions could allow me to see. I started blindly writing letters to the contemplative monasteries for men on the mainland. Even the mainland had few options. I wrote to the Cistercians in country Victoria. Thomas Merton was a Cistercian, though he ended up living as a hermit. I wrote to the Benedictines in New South Wales. Then I finally found an address for Carmelite friars in Middle Park in Melbourne. There was a sense of relief when I found an address for male Carmelites. I noticed the feeling. I suspected it was a sign.

My letters to these mysterious, contemplative worlds were simple requests: I am interested in finding out options for a contemplative vocation. I would appreciate any information you can send about your order.

I sent my letters and I waited. Engineering studies continued. The rhythms of my home life with my parents continued. But I felt my real life was down below the surface. I once wandered through my town stopping at bookshops. Now I walked to churches to pray. I sat silently staring at tabernacles. I fingered my way through the rosary. I went to weekday mass.

I was becoming so seriously catholic, I figured I should go to confession. I had not been for years. I went to my local church one Saturday morning. The place was completely empty but a green light above the door of the large corner confessional indicated the priest was in and ready to receive a penitent. I felt a surge of nerves as I stepped inside and faced my first choice. Should I go old school and kneel behind a screen or go around and sit opposite the priest? I went and sat opposite him. He welcomed me and said an initial prayer. I launched into the usual commencement to confessing.

"Bless me father for I have sinned, it's been a while since my last confession …"

"How long?"

"Well, a couple of years. I'm not sure exactly."

"OK."

"And these are my sins."

I ventured into a litany of struggles and wrongdoings. I stared down at the ground trying to gather up anything worth saying. I finally arrived at the main reason I thought I should confess. I had gone into the confessional feeling something close to grief. It wasn't because of what I was going to confess, but the fact that I had decided, once the confession happened, that I wouldn't commit the so-called sin again. The sense of impending loss was enormous.

"Well, I have masturbated, quite often, um, and well, I've also been going to mass and taking communion without confessing it beforehand."

I said this expecting a mild response, after all I hadn't grown up in a fire-and-brimstone kind of church. I looked up and the priest's normally sedate face had taken on hard angles. His eyebrows merged in a knot of grave concern.

"This is a serious sin. You are aware of the

church's teaching on this?"

"Yes, Father."

"Hmm. How often?"

"Oh, I couldn't really say with certainty. It's been over a number of years."

"Since?"

"Well, I guess since I was about fourteen or so."

He sighed and thought for a moment. I should have felt relief that I had finally said it and absolution would soon be given, but the silence was heavy and awkward.

"For your penance I want you to go and sit before Jesus on the cross and reflect on what you have done to him. Now an act of contrition."

"O my God," I prayed, "I am very sorry that I have sinned against you, because you are so good, and with your help I will not sin again."

The priest raised his hand for the absolution and prayed.

"God the Father of mercies, through the death and resurrection of his Son, has reconciled the world to himself and sent the Holy Spirit among us for the forgiveness of sins; through the ministry of the church may God grant you pardon and peace and I absolve you of your sins in the name of the Father and of the Son and of the Holy Spirit. Amen"

I stepped out of the confessional and sat in the church. I looked up at the strangely golden Jesus on his cross and I thought about the pleasure I was giving up. Sometimes that ecstatic moment of release was the only thing I looked forward to in the day. Now I was sitting in the church to do my penance.

My nocturnal passion had felt good, but it was judged as a ticket to hell if it wasn't confessed. And there was Jesus dead on a cross. Pleasure. Pain. Nails hammered into hands and feet. Forgiveness. My body put in its place. On the shelf. My life set right with God and the church. I was meant to feel forgiven and liberated, and yet I couldn't shake a sense of discord. There was that lingering sense of grief over the loss of future pleasure, but also a suspicion that, whatever just happened, it had nothing much to do with you.

CHAPTER ELEVEN

It was the summer break leading into my final year as an engineering student. I had picked up a temporary job with the Department of Main Roads and was working with a road crew on the Esk Highway in northeast Tasmania. It was simple, repetitive work. We moved along the length of the highway carrying out tests every fifty metres, with a device called a Benkelman Beam, to measure the bounce in the road surface. We hauled the jackhammer off the back of the truck every two hundred metres, then dug test pits and bagged samples from the layers of gravel that made the road.

It felt like an honest day's work with obvious results. There were pages of road deflection measurements and sample bags in the back of the truck waiting to go to the lab. I was surprised how much pleasure I found in the sweat and grime of the work and the good ache in my legs and back at the end of the day. I could do the job without my usual fear that I was on the brink of someone discovering I was a fraud.

I lay on my bed in the evening, in a room above the front bar of the St Mary's Hotel where I was staying. It was an austere room with an old iron-frame bed, a basin and a table in the corner. The window opened onto a balcony with a view of the main intersection in the middle of town, which was usually quiet. The murmur of conversations and occasional surges of laughter drifted through the floorboards from the bar below. The pub's background music had a large measure of Slim Dusty. I didn't mind. I stared up at the ceiling and was glad to feel my bones and muscles settle on a firm mattress after spending all day out on the road. Down below, Slim crooned his love for having a beer with Duncan, and I felt surprisingly content.

That summer brought an unexpected moment of choice. It whispered through the satisfaction I felt in the simple work I was doing. It lingered over me like an afternoon breeze along the Fingal Valley, as I stood with the stop/slow sign controlling non-existent traffic. The older men in the road crew mentioned there was a job vacancy and wondered if I was interested.

"It's there for the taking, young fella," said Bo, who was a bristly potent giant of a man, as strong as an ox, with an extraordinary memory for cricket statistics.

He was keen that I apply for the job. It might have been on account of my over-enthusiastic work ethic. I had a young man's habit of rushing to do the heavy lifting and grunt work to prove myself. But, regardless of his reason for encouraging me, it was good to be liked by an ordinary bunch of blue-collar blokes.

Applying for the job was an absurd idea from the point of view of cold logic. It was the kind of job taken by men who left school at sixteen or younger, and who had no qualifications. I was in my early twenties and less than a year away from gaining an engineering degree. Theoretically, I wasn't far off directing the managers of road crews in the business of maintaining and building roads and bridges. Yet, for a moment, I felt the appeal of taking that job, shrugging off the burden of my education and all the expectations that came with it, and avoiding the indebtedness that would come with a high salary. I allowed myself a moment to imagine this might be enough for me. A simple, working-class life not far removed from the lives of my not-too-distant ancestors. But I knew another life was taking shape inside me. It wasn't a life I could discuss with the men in the road crew. My words would have betrayed me. My sense of blue-collar belonging would have immediately evaporated as the old men shut down to me and categorised me as a smart-arse or a God-botherer or both.

My growing other life came from books and reflection, spirituality and prayer. It was a life of spirit and language waiting to be realised somewhere over there. I just had to find the right place, and then I knew I would finally be right. I would be right in my own skin, and in the world, and with you. I just had to find it: the place where the outside circumstances matched my inside life.

I received replies from the contemplative monasteries I wrote to earlier. Their vocations directors sent back thick envelopes full of brochures and booklets about their religious orders: summaries of their orders' ancient histories, retreat brochures, ministry pamphlets and booklets on the formation processes that made monks of men. It was interesting, though not compelling. Their saints didn't speak to me.

I had written to my cousin to let her know that I

had located the male Carmelites at Middle Park. She replied with surprising speed and gave a hefty shove to assist the grace of my potential vocation. The Middle Park Carmelites were the wrong ones. The male members of her branch of Carmelites, the Discalced or Shoeless Carmelites founded by Saint Teresa, were also in Melbourne but in Box Hill. My cousin suggested the Discalced Carmelite friars might be of more interest to me given my interest and sense of connection with Saint Teresa and Saint John of the Cross. She included a small, brown vocations booklet about the friars and suggested I might want to get in touch with the vocations director. The Box Hill address was at the back of the booklet.

I wrote into the unknown yet again. I provided some details about my connection with the Launceston Carmelites, the books that I had been reading, my attraction to and interest in exploring a vocation. I included the Gethsemane poem and wondered how it might be received. I sealed up the envelope and dropped it into the corner-shop letterbox, with a sense of deja vu. My spiritual destiny seemed to be forever in the hands of Australia Post.

CHAPTER TWELVE

I had no idea what the life of a Discalced Carmelite friar, living at the end of the 1980s, looked like. My impression of contemporary Carmelite life was based on my encounters and correspondence with my nun cousin. How representative was she? Did all Carmelites share her frighteningly thorough fascination with the minutiae of the Pope's life? Did the friars share her interest in a group of Yugoslavian teenagers who were claiming to have daily visions of Mary? Was there any sense of enclosure in the life of the friars? Did they speak with a similar hushed intensity as my cousin?

My only other source of information was the mystic writing of sixteenth-century Spaniards. Their writing conveyed the dynamic energy of a new reform movement. What was the life they envisioned like four centuries later in suburban Melbourne? Were the friars poetic like John? Were they all close to union with God?

A letter arrived in the mail. I looked at the return address on the back: Rev. Christopher O'Dwyer OCD, Priory of Saint John of the Cross, Box Hill.

I took the letter to my bedroom, cut it open with a letter opener, and took out the folded single sheet of paper. The crest of the order and the address was on the top right-hand corner. The handwriting was neat, firm and written with a flow that suggested the use of a fountain pen. I started reading.

"Thank you for your recent letter. I am writing as I was recently appointed the vocations director for our region. I might best answer your question, regarding what our life is like, with some brief examples from my own life.

Last night I had my final shift volunteering with Lifeline. It has been a rewarding but challenging experience. I am currently wrapping up my life in Melbourne. I am doing the rounds and saying my goodbyes. I have finished my studies and was recently ordained. I will soon join the formation community in Sydney. I have been appointed as the assistant novice master for the novitiate due to commence in July next year.

Prayer is certainly the foundation of our lives, as is the case with the nuns. We are not enclosed. That wasn't part of Teresa's vision for the friars. We minister in the community in a variety of ways including running parishes, the retreat centre in Sydney, and working in a range of other areas.

As students we go out to college while the senior members of the community lecture at the college. There is also a place, in our life, for recreation. A number of us recently went to see *Dead Poets Society*. It's worth seeing if you haven't seen it already.

The student master also had a look at your letter and poem. He thought it was interesting and he has suggested you consider coming and visiting our community in Box Hill. In the meantime, keep up the reading and prayer. Kind regards, Chris."

The letter was a revelation. The friars didn't live behind bars. They even went to movies and the fact they went to *Dead Poets Society* augured well. I loved the Robin William's character whispering *carpe diem*, seize the day, in the ears of his young students and another scene when he spun the most uptight boy into a state of frenzied, poetic freedom. My feelings about the movie merged and mingled with the fire-powered poetry of Saint John of the Cross and the life-forging courage of Saint Teresa of Avila. I felt the possibility that a friar's life might be nothing less than a liberating adventure, played out on the big-city canvas of Melbourne, seizing the day in a world supersaturated with ancient meaning, listening to the whisper of Uncle Walt Whitman, the whisper of Spanish saints, all leading to a rich and full life that far outweighed any sacrifice.

CHAPTER THIRTEEN

Word came down from my nun cousin in Launceston. The relatively new Archbishop of Tasmania, Eric D'Arcy, had sent out a request. He wanted to hear peoples' thoughts on the topic of 'The Christian Life and the Search for Happiness'. The nuns had set to work writing their own contribution. "I'm sure you could put together a suitable contribution, Rob," she wrote. "It's been suggested it might be helpful if you read some of the main documents of the Second Vatican Council particularly *Gaudium et Spes*. The Archbishop is most interested in what young people have to offer and I'm sure your contribution would be most welcome."

I was well into my final year of engineering studies and was glad to have a distraction. It was a chance to produce something that mattered. I had absorbed a lot in less than a year: the writing of the Carmelite saints; Thomas Merton's books on contemplation and solitude; the austere beauty of the ancient desert fathers; the Jesus prayer of the Russian pilgrim. Now I was plunging into the bustle of bishops and cardinals hammering out a 1960s Second Vatican Council vision of the modern church. I wanted to absorb it all and feel the points of connection: Good Pope John pushing windows open, fresh air, joy and hope, the murmur of a living past and the promise of a future to believe in.

I sat in the elegant sandstone church in the city to pray. There were often people dropping in to pay a visit, but it was quiet that afternoon. I was alone in the pews. I knelt for a few minutes and then sat. I had too much racing through my mind. My head felt close to bursting. The tension was more palpable in the quiet of the church. The interior was bathed with the same stained-window light that illuminated my paternal great-grandparents when they married there in 1881. My parents married in the same church sixty-eight years later. The intimate traces of my family were even more solidly found a few blocks away, inside the catholic cathedral, in the remaining sections of the original high altar that was carved by my maternal great-grandfather, Bryan Molloy, a stonemason from Tullamore. In these churches, in the church, the personal and profound merged, ethereal as incense, solid as stone.

I looked towards the sanctuary at the altar and tabernacle and the flickering sanctuary candle. I gazed at the drama of Mather Brown's *Resurrection* painting behind the altar with its white child-faced Jesus risen above the fray. I thought about resurrection as visceral as a violent grasp and skyward thrust. Tears started rolling down my cheeks, and I felt a forceful ache in my ribs. The devastation felt sweet. I laid my head on Saint Teresa's shoulder and sobbed, and then I went home and wrote my essay for the Archbishop.

I approached the essay in a similar manner to writing poetry. I sat in the kitchen handwriting scribbled interconnected ideas: the deep searching inclination of human nature; the seemingly unavoidable experience of dissatisfaction; the idea of happiness; the spiritual life, prayer and a deepening relationship with God. I felt pleasure as I wrote. I was using my mind to produce something I was proud to call my own. But there was something else beneath the pride. As my fingers hammered on the keys of my old typewriter and my words smacked down on the page, as the cicadas made a chorus in the front lawn and the river ran through the ancient valley to the south, I inhabited a space that centuries of people had occupied. It was a space of pondering the great questions of life. Writing was an entry point to belonging: a feeling of living connection between the here and now and the deep ancient roots of other people's lives and all their pondering.

I finished the essay and sent it to the Archbishop. He soon invited me to join a young adults' discussion group to be held in his residence. There was another young man in my parish, who had written an essay on the topic. His name was Simon. He was a couple of years younger than me. He was going to the diocesan seminary the following year. Simon rang and offered me a lift to the Archbishop's residence for the meeting. I happily accepted. There was also a young woman, about my age, in the group. The three of us were the sum total of the Archbishop's young adults' discussion group.

"Ah, welcome!" Eric D'Arcy said at the front door.

He invited us to come through to his study. He was a tall man and my hand felt lost in the handshake.

"Hallo, Your Grace," I said.

We walked through a hall and into a room. I

looked around at the many shelves of books. It was a significant academic's study. The Archbishop was educated in Oxford and Rome and had been the head of the Department of Philosophy at Melbourne University before becoming the Bishop of Sale and then the Archbishop of Tasmania. "Have you seen the unfolding events in Tiananmen Square?" he asked. "I just watched the latest coverage. Those brave people gathering the injured onto their bicycles and racing off to the hospital brought to mind my father. He was a medic in the First World War."

He invited us to sit. The housekeeper brought in tea and biscuits. We made small talk for a while. The Archbishop let us know he had been looking forward to the meeting. He missed the vigorous cut and thrust of ideas among young people that he had known and loved as both a student and university lecturer. The conversation lulled so he brought the focus onto our essays.

He invited each of us to share something from what we had written, and he then opened up a discussion of points that seemed particularly significant. My heart swelled when he spoke with enthusiasm about my essay. He wondered if I had studied any theology. I assured him that I had not. I felt slightly stunned. An archbishop had just praised my writing. I could not think of any time in my life when I had experienced that level of validation. My words meant something to an archbishop.

That moment of praise gave me a small taste of a particular power in the church. It's impossible to fully understand the church without considering the experience of patronage. It begins with a handshake and then a conversation that might be reticent, at first, but then gradually becomes more open and trusting as the two find some common cause. There is a light of recognition in the eyes, a glimmer of common understanding, a wry smile and a nod – all suggesting the two people are on the same page when it comes to a certain matter.

The patron has power, but limited time. He is pressed to the end of his days, and not only sees his own death, but the possible death of what he values. The one who receives the patronage, who is taken under the wing, has little power and experience but he does have the luxury of time. He can take up the cause and extend its life into the future. There's trust and loyalty in the relationship, but also a pragmatic, political kind of hope.

These are the relationships that determine everything from the funding priorities in a parish to the election of a pope. All that's best and worst in the church begins in the exchange of patronage.

I had a minor taste of that world of patronage when I sat in that small discussion group with the Archbishop, pondering the connection between faith and happiness. The positive attention and appreciation shown by a powerful man added to my sense that I was moving in the right direction and coming into my own. Simply being in his study, surrounded by his books, gave a measure to the degree and speed of change in my life. I was no longer the isolated boy who envied the conversations of others in the university refectory. I was now sharing my own ideas with a church leader and philosopher, and even going so far as to argue my point with a genuine sense of self-assurance.

CHAPTER FOURTEEN

I was on my way home from university one afternoon. It had been a strange day. My structural engineering lecturer asked me to see him in his office. I had been at university for close to four years, and I had never set foot in a lecturer's office. I could have counted on the fingers of one hand, the number of times I had directly interacted with lecturers.

He was short and bald, with a heavy Eastern European accent, and a quiet, reserved manner. He beckoned me into the room when he saw me at the door.

"Mr Donnelly," he said with a formality that I was not used to hearing. "Thank you for coming. You see, I am most concerned about your work. It makes no sense."

He pulled out one of my assignments to illustrate his point. There were pages of mathematical formulae that I had written and submitted. I recognised my work was equivalent to someone spouting the words of a language that they didn't comprehend. Of course it made no sense. The lecturer looked at me with a perplexed gaze, and I was touched by his concern.

"It's OK," I said to reassure him. "I will never be an engineer. I'm going to become a priest."

It was the first time I declared the intention to anybody. I felt liberated in that moment. I had stretched my wings and suddenly taken flight. Free as a bird. The dark ocean of engineering calculations no longer had a hold on me. My destiny was elsewhere. The lecturer's eyebrows arched in surprise.

This was not the outcome of the conversation that he had calculated. Not even with a large margin of error.

"Well, you might do that, but you should finish this degree. The other thing might not work out."

I thanked him and left. It was the first time a university staff member had expressed a genuine degree of interest and care towards me. It was touching, but no longer relevant. The conversation was still playing through my mind, as I got on the bus in the city to go home. I paid the driver. I turned and saw my old schoolmate, David, sitting in one of the front seats. I hadn't seen him for five or six years.

"Hey," I said, as I sat next to him.

"Hey," he replied.

I had heard some stories about him. After leaving school early, he tried a few jobs but none of them worked out. There was talk that he was taking to the bush frequently, wandering on the fringes of the suburbs, and that all of this was evidence that he was seriously depressed. I could see there was a weight around his eyes. He was far from the carefree kid who walked beside me on adventures through the hills of West Hobart when we were in primary school.

Every attempt at conversation on the bus that afternoon disintegrated into a thick silence. His eyes were vacant even when he looked at me. My words didn't seem to register at all. He had fallen into some dark emptiness, and the gravity of it scared me.

I was running to catch the afternoon bus a few weeks later. I caught sight of him on the bus. I deliberately slowed my pace and let the bus take off without me. I don't know if he saw me. I don't think he did. But I saw the petty treachery in myself, and I've never stopped seeing it.

We shared the usual morbid curiosity of young boys in those days when we took the long routes through the suburbs to our primary school. One time our conversation turned towards the bridge that spanned the river with its high arch. We were boys from the eastern shore, so the bridge was strong in our imaginations. A ship had ploughed into its pylons a few years before and brought down the highest span. The lights went out along the length of the bridge. Cars kept driving into the dark. They went over the broken edge and plummeted sixty metres to the water below. The bridge was our first evidence that the solid world can break.

"Do you think they were dead before they hit the water?" David asked.

"I dunno," I said, as we turned a corner towards school.

I don't know how it was for him when he fell. They didn't find his body. A passing driver saw someone, matching his description, climb the rails. Next minute he was gone. He wasn't the first school mate to commit suicide, and he wouldn't be the last. The solid world can break. It does. Some boys barely made it into adult life before they died.

What do you say to that? What have you ever said to that? Where is the voice to tell the stories they never had a chance to tell?

I made a vow at his memorial service. I would

never betray a friend again. If a future friend came into my life, I would stand by him no matter what occurred. I would reach out regardless of my own discomfort. I would be loyal. I would make kindness the measure of my life.

Did I want to be like you or was I just trying to fill the space made by your absence?

It was an over-reaching, redemption-seeking vow. It would keep me honest, but it also pressed seeds of regret into my future.

CHAPTER FIFTEEN

I was seventeen when I first travelled to mainland Australia. I went with my parents. We flew out the day after my final exam for the year. I had one more year of school ahead of me and then university. It was the first time I had been on a plane. I was invited to take a look in the cockpit and say hallo to the pilots. I felt awkward. I imagined I was too old for that sort of indulgence, but I visited the cockpit anyway.

We spent a few days in Melbourne, went on a tour of the Melbourne Cricket Ground, wandered around the Queen Victoria Market, and were side-tracked on a mission to see if manufacturers in the big smoke had better quality material for Mum's apron-making business than the local suppliers in Hobart. I was mesmerised by the size of the city. I walked along the streets with my head tilted back. I did not want to miss any part of the place. The size and energy was so extraordinary, it felt like I was walking through an intense dream.

The mainland trip was planned in detail. We travelled by bus along the Great Ocean Road, stopping at Portland overnight, and then we went on to Mount Gambier and finally Adelaide. One small step for most people was a giant leap for me. I took photos and collected souvenirs at every stop, as though I was gathering evidence to prove the mainland really existed and I had really been there. We stayed in Adelaide for a few days, and then caught a train across the Nullarbor Plain to Perth to spend time with my oldest brother Rick.

The unending flat of the desert was as startling as Melbourne. There was nothing but stumpy scrub and a flat, red-rimmed horizon and then one or two houses in the middle of nowhere, and people standing out the front to wave at the passing train.

We stopped in Kalgoorlie and I went for a walk on my own. Some women, out the front of a brothel, called out to me in a good-natured way: "Hey sweetheart. Give you a discount!" I blushed and smiled, then walked back to the train. It was the closest I had ever been to having a sexual encounter.

I was twenty-two when I travelled to mainland Australia for the second time. It was December 1989 and I travelled on my own. It was an entirely different kind of adventure. I was on a plane to Melbourne to see if I could find my future. The young Carmelite priest, Chris, who had corresponded with me, met me. He was in a neat polo shirt and pants. He gave me a measured smile, and then there was an awkward moment that resulted in something between a handshake and a hug.

We went down to claim my luggage.

"Well, it's good that you have come when you did, though I won't be here for long," he said. "I'm flying to Perth first thing tomorrow. I'm helping in our parish over Christmas. After that I will be in Varroville."

"That's the Sydney retreat centre?"

"Yes. There's the retreat centre and also a parish. It's in the south-west. Do you know Sydney?"

"No. I've never been there."

"Oh," he said. "Well, here we are. Did you have much baggage? I wouldn't imagine you do."

"No, just one small bag."

"Carry-on's always best for short trips. It saves the bother of waiting around."

I claimed my bag, and we made our way to the car after paying for the parking. The car was relatively new. We were soon in the flow of traffic. It seemed heavy for four in the afternoon. It was certainly heavy by Hobart standards. I would have been happy to just absorb the unfolding sights of Melbourne, but I knew this was a time for making a good impression and finding out information. I was also nervous. I was in a car with a Carmelite friar on the way to stay in a monastery. I had thrown myself into most extraordinary circumstances.

"Is the student house close to the centre of the city?"

"It's about fifteen kilometres, give or take. It's a fairly quick drive."

"And how many students are there?"

"In the student house?"

"Yes."

"We've just had three solemn professions and two ordinations. There's two simply professed students and two postulants. There's an aspirant in Sydney, some other nibbles that may or may not come to anything, and well there's yourself too."

"What's an aspirant?"

"Someone who's seriously looking at joining the order."

"Oh. So, vocations-wise, how do the Carmelites compare with other orders?"

"Quite well. The Dominicans in Camberwell have students. The Redemptorists have a few. The Blessed Sacraments likewise. The Divine Word Missionaries are in quite a good state. They're our nearest neighbours. Just across the road. Of course, some congregations haven't had a vocation in years."

"That's a shame," I said, thinking that was the appropriate response.

"Not necessarily," Chris replied. "We're in a time of significant change. Religious life is no exception. That's why it's so important to have a decent grasp of history. Change creates opportunities for adaptation, innovation. Old ways die. New forms of life rise." There was a moment of awkward silence.

"And there's a novitiate coming up soon?" I asked.

"Yes, probably commencing in July in Sydney. I think I mentioned I will be assistant novice master. Of course, I anticipate I will be taking on the bulk of the formation work. Paddy, the novice master, is going to stay on as parish priest as well. I'm hoping to achieve some progress with the liturgy in Sydney. God love the Irish. They're by and large a good mob, in their way, but they don't have a great concern with beautiful worship. We need that. There's a place for bells and smells in the church."

I sat in the car and listened to an ongoing monologue that ranged from the importance of historical criticism to the rich heritage of Judaism to the important agenda of ecumenism. I was bewildered by most of what he was saying, perplexed by his strange terminology, and had no idea how to respond appropriately. But I was glad he had a lot to say. I was able to sit quietly. Listening. Absorbing. I nodded and made noises of interest as I stole glances at the great sprawl of Melbourne, with the hope of seeing at least one tram during the car trip. I asked questions where it seemed warranted, and then he launched into speech again.

The quick weave along rapid multi-lane roads, the constant horn blasts, the rumble of trucks, the flash of trains at level-crossings, and the overall magnitude of the place was foreign to me. It was strange that my desire for a contemplative life had brought me to such a busy place.

We came along a road where shops had Chinese writing and little hint of English. It was fascinating. I really was in a foreign world and a long way from home. We turned into a quiet street. It had a reassuring suburban familiarity. After a block of flats, there were normal houses with front yards. Gnarled plane trees lined the street, creating a summer-green canopy above. I drank it in. It stilled me. I felt alright.

The monastery was towards the end of the street. It was a compact place of orange bricks with red tiled roofs. Its double-storey accommodation wing adjoined another wing that had communal spaces: a large kitchen, a dining room and a somewhat dishevelled lounge room. The chapel sat prominently in the foreground of the monastery.

Chris bustled me into the accommodation wing. He referred to the bedrooms as cells. I was assigned to one, downstairs, next to an apparently hibernating priest who I was told not to disturb under any circumstances. I was briefly alone. I tried to steady my dizzy head and gain some sense of orientation. The room was spacious with a bed, a sink and built-in wardrobes. There were warm carpet tiles on the floor and a generous-sized window that faced onto the garden.

I barely settled before Chris reappeared to tell me it was time for evening prayer. He was now dressed in the brown habit of a Carmelite friar. He wore a long-belted tunic overlaid by a straight-edged front and back panel, called a scapular, and a hooded top piece, called a capuche.

We walked across to the chapel and entered its white interior. The two long walls were lined with wooden choir chairs. The two lines of chairs faced each other, rather than towards the square block altar at the far end. There was a silver overlaid icon of the Madonna on the left wall. An oil lamp that sometimes flickered and sent up a thin line of smoke illuminated it. There was a black box tabernacle directly behind the altar. It was partly peeled back to suggest a hidden interior of gold. A cross, with a weathered Christ, hung above the altar.

I looked around and recognised the symbols. They were straight out of the poetry and prose I had been absorbing for months. A thin line of stained glass, at the top of the side walls, had images of John of the Cross's *Spiritual Canticle*. A round window, above the door, featured the vibrantly enflamed heart from the *Living Flame* poem. It was the first moment, in my brief mainland adventure, when I recognised elements that quietly and reassuringly made sense.

I took a seat and watched as a strange assortment of men entered. Some were in habits, while others were in ordinary clothes. Some stole glances at me, and then went about their business extracting books from underneath their seats. A tall friar walked to the altar and lit two long candles in the front. Chris gave me a book and encouraged me to join in. I noticed everyone was standing and facing towards the altar, so I did the same and then a soft voice behind me started the prayers.

"O God, come to our aid."

"O Lord, make haste to help us," all replied.

The two sides turned to face each other and bowed.

"Glory be to the Father and to the Son and to the Holy Spirit," chanted one side.

"As it was in the beginning, is now, and ever shall be, world without end. Amen," replied the other.

There was a hymn. All sat and the recitation of psalms began. One side chanted one stanza. The opposite side chanted the next. Their monotone voices flattened the rolling emotional landscape of the words. I noticed the shortest friar's intonation had the growling quality of electric shears stripping a sheep of its wool.

I followed as best I could, trying to pick up the cues of others, and frequently coming undone. This elicited occasional amused smiles, particularly from a Chinese-looking friar who sat opposite me. The man who had started the prayers leaned over to me when I had clearly lost my place. He pointed at the appropriate section, patted my arm, and then sat back and continued praying.

There was silent prayer after evening prayer. I went back to my room, or cell, where I sat on the floor and flicked through a book on Elizabeth of the Trinity, a beatified French Carmelite nun. I liked her wide, sad eyes and felt I'd like to know more about her. I waited in the room and wondered what everyone else was doing. I figured it wasn't right to go exploring, so I stayed in the room until there was a knock on the door.

"Come in," I said.

A tall, young man in a light blue T-shirt and jeans came in. "You're sitting on the floor," he said with a touch of concern.

"Yeah, I often sit on the floor."

"Oh! Anyway, I'm Julian."

"Rob, pleased to meet you." I got up and shook his hand.

"It's time to eat. Follow me. So, you're from Tassie?"

"Yeah."

"How are you finding the place?"

"It's very different."

"Different from how you imagined?"

"I don't really know yet."

I followed Julian along the hall and downstairs into the kitchen. It was a large space with a bench and sink below a row of windows that looked out on a tree-lined driveway. There was a table in the centre of the room, a large gas-top oven to the right, and a fridge in the corner. There was a separate pantry. It seemed like a dark, exotic space, full of mysterious foreign bottles on shelves, and bags of rice laid on the floor like sandbags.

The friars were milling about in the kitchen. One was putting food on a sideboard that was open to a dining room. Others were chatting. My impression was that most of the men were in their late twenties or early thirties. Julian was about my age or possibly younger.

There was one man standing in the corner. His habit was cinched tight at the waist, showing he was trim, but his receding hair suggested he was older than the others. He watched the dinner preparation and the general milling about of the group as though from a slight distance. He was there, but not quite there – an observer of the busy world around him.

I was immediately engaged in a conversation with the Chinese-looking friar who had sat opposite me during prayer.

"So, you're from Tasmania?" he asked.

"I sure am."

"I'm Sam."

"Rob."

We shook hands.

"So," he said, then cleared his throat and sniffed, "do you come from a big family?"

"I'm the youngest of five."

"How many brothers and sisters?"

"One sister. She's the oldest and then three brothers."

"And they're all in Tassie?"

"Well yes, most, I have a brother in Perth."

"So, you've settled in? Which room?" he continued with little pause for breath.

"The bottom floor up the far end."

"Ah ... next to Finch. Good. Good," he cleared his throat again. "Well, this is the true heart of the student house," he said gesturing to the kitchen. "It's where cooking and theologising happens. That's what a student house is all about — food and conversation — wouldn't you say so Father Ryan?"

"Well, to some extent, Sam," the man in the corner said with a somewhat indifferent air.

"And I've heard you've been involved in a discussion group with Eric D'Arcy?" Sam continued.

"Yes. I wrote an essay and then there was a discussion group on the topic."

"He was a significant presence at Melbourne Uni. I'm studying there," he said, suddenly changing conversational tack.

"Oh. What are you studying?"

"Philosophy. I'm doing my Masters, for all my sins." He pushed his glasses up and crinkled his nose.

"Right, time to eat," interjected a no-nonsense potbellied man with a beard.

A queue formed in the dining room. I introduced myself to the other friars, as we served ourselves from a range of dishes. I was reassured to see meat was on the menu. I had a vague idea Carmelites didn't eat meat.

"Hallo. Robert is it?" asked the short friar I had noticed in the chapel. "I'm Checkers. Half Chinese, half Czech." He giggled, and I smiled. "Welcome.

You're very welcome."

"Hi Robert. I'm Peter," said the tall friar who I had noticed lighting the candles in the chapel before prayer. He was just behind me in the queue.

"Hi. So, are you a student too?" I asked.

"Well, I was, but this is my last night. I'm leaving tomorrow."

"Oh. Are you being posted somewhere else?"

"No. I'm leaving the order," he said, then calmly elaborated. "The time came for taking final vows. I took some further time to discern and came to see this isn't the life for me."

I found a seat at the long table in the midst of this group of men. There was some conversation, but most focused on the serious business of eating. Julian and Checkers were particularly quiet through the meal, though Julian looked over at me at one stage.

"Have you spent much time in Melbourne?" he said.

"Only once when I was seventeen and that was just for a couple of days."

"Maybe we could go into the city tomorrow? Is that OK, Father Ryan?"

"Sure Julian," the priest said.

I listened to the chatter. I could hear Chris, at the far end of the table, talking through the logistics of getting to the airport in the morning for his flight to Perth. Ryan was quietly talking to Peter who was sitting by his side. I wondered what was being said. What was it like to spend so many years in an order, and then leave? He seemed such a peaceful man.

How could he not belong in a place like this?

Sam broke my line of thought. He was discussing finer points about the food that he was eating.

"We all take turns cooking here, Rob," he said to me. "At least once a week, sometimes more. Can you cook?"

"Mostly casseroles."

"Ah ... Mum's cooking?" Ryan said. His unexpected interaction surprised me. I felt like he had hardly noticed me at all.

"Well, yes, I guess so."

"Tasmanian food to add to the international cuisine of the house," Sam enthused.

The meal finished, then some went back to the kitchen while others wandered off. I stepped in to help dry dishes. The potbellied man started washing the crockery and cutlery with calamitous vigour. Everything crashed down into the drying rack. I was surprised things weren't broken in the process. He didn't seem overly interested in conversation, so I settled into work.

"If you can't find where things go, you can leave them on the table," he said.

Chris invited me to his cell for a conversation once I finished drying up. He had an almost full suitcase on the bed and boxes on the floor. He gestured to a seat and then thrust a book into my hands.

"I have to go and make some calls. It's just been a mad time wrapping things up here. The parishioners gave me that book as part of a farewell gift. Some of them know me far too well! It really is most amusing," he said, as he walked out of the room.

I stared at the closing door then looked down and found I was holding a pop-up book about the Royal Family. I sat in the room looking at that most peculiar book, with its three-dimensional pictures of the Queen, her corgis and assorted other royals. I wondered how I could begin to make sense of this bewildering place. Who was this man I had been uncovering my soul to, in letters, all these months? He seemed frantic, and I felt my arrival was an inconvenience to him. And why was the tall, peaceful man leaving the order? He was exactly the sort of person I imagined I would find in a monastery. And what was the story with the mysterious Father Ryan, who seemed to be the gravitational centre of the place? And what about the hibernating priest next door to my room? What was the story there? Why had there been such an emphasis on not disturbing him? I had questions but no answers, and no clear sense that this was the place where I was meant to be.

CHAPTER SIXTEEN

The next day began with mass and morning prayer. I left the monastery with Julian after breakfast. We crossed the road, walked through the suburb, and came out near a train line. I noticed a stonemason near the entrance to a cemetery. There was a tattoo parlour further along the road. We took a pedestrian crossing over the line. There was a library on the other side and a TAFE college. I could see the train line went below a main road and a shopping centre that was up ahead.

"The station is underneath the shops," Julian said. "We just need to get a ticket."

The train tickets resembled instant lotto cards.

"We have to scratch out the right sections. It's a new system. We should scratch it for all-day travel," Julian explained.

I was surprised at a system that relied on everyone being honest and scratching the appropriate squares. Julian said a lot of people ripped off the system, but the fines were hefty if you were caught.

We went downstairs to the station platform. It was dark apart from a blue screen suspended from the roof. It gave details about the next train arriving. I looked up, saw the next train was to the city, and felt a surge of excitement. I now had the chance to see Melbourne.

It was good to be out in the wide world and have a break from the monastery. I had been there for less than twenty-four hours and my head was already crammed full of too many perplexing impressions to decipher.

"Have you always lived in Melbourne?" I asked Julian.

"Yes, well, since I left school. I grew up in Bacchus Marsh. I was in the diocesan seminary for a while. That didn't work out. I worked as a hospital orderly after that. Now I'm here."

"And it's going alright?"

"So far so good. There is certainly a commitment to community prayer. Far more than the seminary, but that's not saying much. In the seminary, psychology's taken the place of any decent sense of spirituality. It is all enneagrams and Myers-Briggs tests and just a token amount of prayer life. That's not on – well, not for me anyway. Ah, here's our train," he said, as a gust of warm air pushed through the station.

We boarded and found a seat. The train accelerated out of the dark and into the daylight: a careworn silver streak rattling along the line. There was a tree-lined ridge buffering suburbia on the left and the back end of graffiti-tagged office blocks on the right. We accelerated and then slowed to stop at a succession of stations: Mont Albert, Surrey Hills, Chatham, East Camberwell, Camberwell.

Doors opened. Every kind of person got on and off the train. An old woman with a Zimmer frame, a man chatting to his friend in Mandarin, kids playing 'Funky Cold Medina' on a ghetto-blaster. Doors closed. Whistles blew. It was my first experience catching a suburban train. I was fascinated but kept my excitement under wraps.

The stations became larger and busier. The train lines wove and spread like strands of spaghetti passing alongside multiple platforms with increasing numbers of people. I saw a sign: Glenferrie Station. My heart skipped a beat. My football team's traditional home ground was Glenferrie. They didn't play games there anymore. It was too small to be financially viable. A possible religious vocation was one thing but actually being in Glenferrie was something else. I remembered when I watched games on television in the 1970s that the ground was right beside a train line. Was this the train line? Were we going to pass the ground? I looked out the window and there it was below: a pressed-in, little ground with a squat, brick grandstand at the far goal end. I smiled but didn't say anything to Julian.

"It won't be long before we're in the city. I think we should go around the loop. Maybe get off at Parliament," he said.

I was happy to have any experience of the place. The thought of going down through tunnels thrilled me. I looked out and my eyes widened as we passed through Richmond Station.

"Is that the MCG?" I asked, as I pointed at the large stadium up ahead.

"Yeah, are you into footy?"

"A bit. What about you?"

"No. Not really."

We came into an enormous covered space. I had heard people say, all my life, that busy situations were like Flinders Street Station. I looked at the spread of platforms, the clumps of people waiting to go somewhere else, some reading papers, some gazing into the middle distance, others sprinting to catch one train or another. The air was full of a barely decipherable announcement and whistles signalling departures. Our train moved on, passed the Yarra River, shuddered around a corner, and then arrived at Spencer Street Station.

"We're going down into the loop after this," Julian said.

Suddenly we dropped into the dark. The close proximity of the tunnel walls amplified the train's sound. The only thing to see in the window was the illuminated train interior. I looked at myself. I was really in this place. This was what it meant to be in a big city, rushing through tunnels, emerging into the striking bright of underground stations.

We arrived at Parliament Station and got off the train. We walked to escalators. I looked up. There didn't seem to be an end to the ascent. I must have shown surprise.

"Yeah!" Julian said, with a flash of hometown pride. "Longest escalators in the Southern Hemisphere."

"Wow," I said. "How deep are we?"

Julian shrugged. We started the ascent. The contrast between the sleek, shiny world of the underground and the surface world of sunlight, towers and great rivers of traffic was striking. There was bustle everywhere. I heard a rattle, spun around, and saw an approaching tram.

"Well, I know I'm in Melbourne now," I shyly said. Julian beamed back at me.

"So, have you been to Saint Patrick's Cathedral?" he asked.

I shook my head.

We started walking up a road. I could see the cathedral spires pushing skyward. There were traces of familiar sandstone, mainly in the spires, but most of the building was bluestone. It gave the structure a dark impenetrable weight. It was enormous and mysterious. The cathedral in Hobart was a tiny thing in comparison.

I followed Julian through a side door, dipped my hand in the holy water font, made the sign of the cross, then genuflected. Julian moved through the place with an ease that suggested he was born to it. My every step stirred a stumbling wonder in me. I had entered a neo-gothic dream of shadows and stone, whose grand depth was illuminated with golden light from windows that ran down the main body of the cathedral.

Julian pointed back over my head. I turned around.

"That's the Great West Window," he said. "It's the Ascension. You can see Mary and the Apostles below Jesus."

I turned and saw a great stained-glass window. It was actually a cluster of windows: seven long, vertical glass panels displaying the drama of Jesus' heaven-bound departure with smaller panels, above, forming a kind of mandala. The sun-bright, multicoloured work was elegantly framed in ribbons of stone.

"It's beautiful," I said.

We walked down the central aisle past wooden pews and stone columns. "If you look up you can see angels," Julian said.

I looked towards the roof. Beautifully carved timberwork was punctuated by a line of angels, hands solemnly pressed, looking down from on high. Heaven was above. Earth was below. It was architecture made to evoke mystery.

We arrived in front of the sanctuary. The central marble altar seemed small inside the wider elevated space, as though the business of religion itself was close to nothing in that emptiness. Something was there. Something and nothing. It was pooled to a voluminous weight within those great stone walls. I could have sat there for hours wanting nothing more than to be conquered and lost in its immensity. I drew back from it when I saw Julian was already moving on.

He pointed to an elaborate chair on the right. "That's the Archbishop's Cathedra."

"Oh," I said somewhat lost in the terminology, "Who's the Archbishop?"

"Frank Little."

His name wasn't familiar. The church in Melbourne was an unknown world to me apart from my sketchy knowledge of the Irish archbishop, Daniel Mannix, who canvased against conscription in the First World War and supported the Cold War movement of Bob Santamaria after the Second World War. I had little interest in the who's who of the church world in Melbourne or anywhere else for that matter. My interest was elsewhere. We wandered behind the sanctuary. Julian explained this was the ambulatory. There were smaller altars around the back. He said there was a time when priests said individual masses, sometimes simultaneously, at those altars. He shared his knowledge about this sacramental business with a great deal of enthusiasm. I tried to match it with an equal degree of interest but, deep down, all I wanted was to surrender to the magnitude of the place. I suspected everything that mattered was in that magnitude and the ache it woke inside me.

I was glad when we were back outside. The greater surrender wasn't going to happen today. Sun warmth and fresh air brought me back to earth. I relaxed. I breathed deep. We went back towards the central business district.

"We'll go down Collins Street," Julian said. "I'll show you the best view in Melbourne. It's a bit of a strange place for a view, but it's worth it."

There were twin towers at the upper end of Collins Street. I followed Julian into an elevator.

"We'll have to go quickly," Julian said, as we stepped into a deserted restaurant. It looked closed. I could see one of the staff setting tables some distance away.

Julian bolted past tables and straight into a male bathroom. It was a strange contrast after wandering through a nineteenth-century cathedral. I followed him anyway. There was a predictable row of clean sinks with gold fittings, toilet cubicles and urinals. I looked around and saw an almost floor to ceiling window with a magnificent view of the city.

"See. I told you it was worth it," he said with another flash of hometown pride. "It's the best view in Melbourne. These are some of the tallest towers."

We returned to ground level and wandered down Collins Street. We stopped at McDonalds for lunch. Julian seemed to enjoy being tour guide. He was also interested to find out more about me.

"Is it what you imagined?" he asked, after finishing off his burger.

"I'm looking for contemplative life, and there's definitely prayer happening with the Carmelites. I mean it's kind of confusing with the complicated liturgies, but the quiet prayer is really good. And I've been reading a lot of Saint Teresa and John of the Cross. I really love their writing."

"Yeah. The order has a rich tradition: great saints; great teaching; a commitment to prayer. It seems good to me. It's certainly better than the seminary. I hope it can stay faithful to what it's meant to be. There's a lot that's been lost in the church. Do you think you'll join?"

"I'm not sure."

"I hope you do."

He liked me. I liked him too. I knew if I came back, we would become friends. I followed him across the city. There was a great energy and enthusiasm in him. He obviously loved Melbourne along with having a fierce devotion to the church. He talked about some orders with disdain. They had sold out, lost their way, and forgotten the vision of their founding saints. I had no idea what to say when he ventured into that territory. I was wary of church politics. It felt like a jarring antithesis to the thing I felt inside the cathedral.

CHAPTER SEVENTEEN

"Come on Rob, let's have a chat," Ryan said after the evening meal. I followed him up the stairs to the top floor of the accommodation wing. His room was at the far end beside a small telephone room. Ryan had the position of student master in the monastery. He was also a theology lecturer at the neighbouring college.

He invited me into his room. Books were piled on tables, on the floor, even covering his bed. There were periodicals and journals spread around. He ushered me in with no self-consciousness about the academic clutter. He cleared space on a ragged recliner chair, so I could sit down.

It seemed a strangely chaotic space for such a measured man. He sat in another threadbare chair facing me and casually tucked his legs underneath himself. Everything about him suggested unhurried calm.

"So," he said, "you've had some time here now, Rob. Granted a brief time, but still time to see and experience. How have you found your stay with us?"

"Good," I said trying to match his calm tone. "Thanks for having me. It's been interesting. It seems to be quite busy with people coming and going."

"You mean Chris and Peter?"

"Yes, I guess so."

"Well, that's worth reflecting on," he said, as he tilted his head in consideration. "In the case of Chris, well, he – like all of us here, and indeed in our other communities – goes where he is sent by virtue of obedience. This is the practical living out of our vocation, life given over to Christ ... ah ... realised in the practical call to serve the needs of the order and indeed the church; the need to help in our Perth parish; the need to minister in the retreat centre. In the case of Peter – there we have a different, but equivalently authentic, realisation of surrender. Surrender to the spirit through the day-to-day unfolding of discernment, which is right and proper during a time of formation: being true to what comes to be known ... ah ... being rightly disposed and available to that truth through prayer, through discernment. It is openness to that sense of rightness, given in time. Ultimately, for some, that rightness is to stay, while for others it's to go and serve in other ways, in other forms of life."

"How do you know what God's will is?" I asked.

"The disposition that develops through prayer is certainly foundational. Put simply it's the quiet turning to God who dwells within. How is prayer for you?"

"I pray every day. I go to mass most days. I've been reading the work of the Carmelite saints. There's a lot that I find moving in their writing. I feel a sense of connection."

"Well, there's a start. When we speak of charism, the sense of the Spirit making us for this place in the church, the experience is indeed one of relationship. I pick up Teresa, and there is a real sense that she speaks to me and ... ah ... in some ways speaks for me. It's different from intellectual engagement with an idea presented in a book. In the case of charism, it is an intimate exchange, not so much a sharing of an idea, or finding a common interest or concern, but an exchange which is nothing less than a sharing of life. There's charism. Indeed, there is God's will. A call to that fullness of life promised by God, realised in Christ, and brought to fruition in and through the community of the church."

The conversation meandered through Carmelite writing that had resonated with me. Ryan sprang off my insights and pushed the consideration deeper. Ideas were taken up and viewed from various angles as though they were prisms spilling a spectrum of wondrous light. Language mattered. The roots of words mattered. The alternative interpretations of words mattered. A well-chosen phrase was something to be relished. An incomplete line of thought was a challenge to be met.

He punctuated his reflections with a prolonged 'ah ...' when he was reaching for the right word to capture the next idea. His hands took over to complement or compensate for the inadequacies of words. A flat palm pressed through the air denoted the movement towards transcendence, the great other, the beyond.

I felt like I was being taken somewhere in the conversation. I concentrated on his lines of thought, but there was something mesmerising in his tone. I struggled between focused engagement and a mindless surrender to the flow of his verbal pondering. He wasn't like any priest I had ever met. I thought he was the most spiritual person I had ever met.

The conversation clattered back to earth when

Ryan reminded me that a novitiate was soon to commence, there were no plans for another in the near future, and he wondered if I might be ready to join?

I said I wasn't sure.

I flew back to Hobart in a state of panic, promise and paralysis. What was I supposed to do now? What was this absurd mustard seed of resistance inside me? Everything pointed towards entering the monastery. My poetry had been taken over by Jesus. My mind had come alive writing a paper for an archbishop. I had Spanish saints whispering in my ears with a wisdom that I craved. Surely everything I wanted was there: in that rich, living world of spirituality, in the mesmerising drift of the student master's words, in the stillness of prayer and the rhythm of that life, in the promise of community and some ultimate sense of belonging.

If I didn't enter the monastery then what? Engineering? What a joke. I might as well apply for a job as a brain surgeon as an engineer. There was no truth in it. There was no rightness in it. And if not engineering, then what? Where else was there any genuine sense of significance or promise or sign of a life worth living? One thing was certain. I wanted a life, and I wanted it to be solid and true. I wanted something more than mere endurance. What the hell was I doing back in Hobart?

Word came down from on high, via the Launceston nuns. The prior of the Sydney community of friars was visiting them over Christmas. My nun cousin described him as a great biblical scholar and retreat master. She encouraged me to come up and meet him while there was a chance. The need for a speedy resolution regarding my vocation seemed to be thick in the air.

Jimmy was clean shaven with grey woolly hair and red flushed cheeks. He had a soft Irish accent and a great smile that set me at ease. We had lunch together in a small room in the nun's monastery. It was a three-course meal prepared by the nuns and brought to us by the extern: vegetable soup made from their garden produce that hadn't been decimated by the possum, a solid meat-and-three-veg main course, and an old-fashioned dessert that I guessed was sago pudding.

"So, how did you find our student house?" he asked.

"The friars were very welcoming."

"Sure, Ryan's a good man to have there, and we have some fine students coming through. So, you're interested in the order yourself?"

"Well, yes. I guess I'm discerning. Trying to work out God's will."

"You know there's a lot to be said for seeing the life as it's lived. Books are fine, but you need to experience the reality of the life to see if it's right. Robert, you would be welcome to come and spend time with the Sydney community. Get your timing right, and you can join one of our retreats."

"That sounds good. I think I will. Thanks."

He went on to outline his role as the retreat director. He was enthusiastic about the range of retreats now on offer. They ranged from weekends on Carmelite spirituality through to Taize retreats that he said were particularly popular. I could see, after my time in Melbourne and this meal with Jimmy, there was no such thing as a typical Carmelite. They were as diverse a group of men as I had ever come across. We said goodbye, after the meal, and he repeated his invitation to come to Sydney.

CHAPTER EIGHTEEN

It wasn't long before I was on a plane to Sydney. I had never been there. I was met at the airport by a tall man. He was probably in his early to mid-thirties.

"I'm Errol," he said, as he shook my hand.

"I hope you don't mind, but I have to deliver something before we go back to the retreat centre," he said, as we walked away from the arrivals gate.

He had a bouncing Kiwi accent and seemed to choose his words with a tentative deliberation.

"Sure. No problem," I said.

We drove out of the airport. The first thing that struck me was the humidity. It clung to my skin until the air-conditioner gained the upper hand. Traffic was funnelled along narrow winding roads in multiple directions – intricate veins of movement and noise around the rim of Botany Bay and into the thick body of the city. There was a cluster of billboards near the airport entrance. They were glossy signs with beautiful holiday scenes: stylish people with perfect bodies, high-end cars, champagne flutes saluting the sun. Image. Lifestyle. Success. All of it elevated and floodlit along a roadside thick with truck fumes and irritable drivers. Welcome to Sydney.

Errol was quiet. I was happy to let him concentrate on driving. I didn't feel I had to ask questions. He seemed the sort who preferred quiet. He started talking while we waited for a traffic light to change.

"So, you were in our Melbourne house," he said.

"Yes. Just for a few days."

"And how did you find it?"

"Good. They seemed like a friendly community."

"Did you meet Finch?"

"No," I said, remembering the presence of the hibernating priest in the room beside mine. "I think he was there, but he seemed to be kind of keeping to himself or something."

"Well, if you join, you need to watch him. Just be careful of him. He can make a student's life hell on earth if he decides he doesn't like you."

I was taken by surprise. It was the first hint of something dark about life in the order. I told Errol that I would keep his advice in mind, but in my thoughts, I decided to make my own assessment of this man called Finch if I joined. He certainly seemed to be the stuff of legend among the friars. Sam had provided a brief impersonation of the man when I was in Melbourne. His impersonation suggested the mysterious priest was a man of intense, teeth-clenched mutterings laced with explicit emphasis, who was inclined to trot out stories about whores with golden hearts.

"Were you based in Melbourne?" I asked with the suspicion Errol's views were based on his own experience.

"For a while but I'm in Sydney now. I work on the farm."

"Oh, what kind of farm?"

"We have cattle. Meat rather than dairy. We sell the calves."

"Are you a priest or a brother?"

"A brother."

We drove for a while in silence, and then he announced that we were in Coogee. We drove up a hill and turned into a driveway. We walked to the entrance and were greeted by a Carmelite nun. She welcomed us in and then a swarm of Carmelite nuns gathered around. I did a double-take. There was no sign of bars anywhere. They were free-range nuns.

There was a feeling of great affection between the nuns and Errol. He seemed more at ease with them than with me. He even joked with a couple of older nuns who looked like they were twins. A little old nun came up to me.

"We watch the planes come in to land," she said with wide-eyed wonder. "They line up all in a row over the ocean and come in when the airport's ready for arrivals. It's really busy in the early morning. We can hear them going over our roof."

A younger nun with dark, curled hair came over to me. "All of this might be a bit overwhelming for you," she said.

There was a careworn kindness in her eyes, and I liked her straightaway. She wasn't like my cousin. This nun had the down-to-earth manner of someone who was country born and bred. I reassured her that I was OK and asked if this place was a Carmelite monastery. She explained the current community was a combination of two previous communities in Parkes and Dulwich Hill. The two Carmels had decided to merge. They were staying in Coogee while their new monastery was being built next door to the friars' retreat centre. They were looking forward to finally moving into their new home.

There was something poignant about that first stop in Sydney. If I had walked out of the gate where the Carmelite nuns were staying and looked across the nearby intersection of Dudley Street and Mount Street, then I would have seen a ramshackle double-storey building that had once seen better days. And if I looked across that intersection, ten years into the future, then I would have seen my future self walking into that building with a few bags and an ungainly cardboard box. I would have seen Errol, looking the same as when I first met him, helping me with the move. The twenty-two-year-old boy, thick in the tussle of discerning his destiny, would have wondered what it was all about and probably with a measure of alarm. *What happened? What was I doing moving into a place like that? How could my life result in such a scene?*

But the future doesn't speak to the past. If it does, I don't know how. Maybe you do. Maybe you amuse yourself, making patterns out of lives, weaving significance around certain places. A boy's brief visit to some nuns, before going to visit a monastery, crossed paths with a future man's shaky emergence from a monastery into a new life. A decade of my life would amount to one enormous circle. But I had no idea as I said goodbye to the nuns and got back in the car.

The retreat centre was in a suburb called Varroville in South Western Sydney. We drove along roads that slashed through the suburbs. I wondered how people lived surrounded by so much noise. I recognised some names on the street signs: Parramatta, Liverpool, Bankstown, Ingleburn. I wondered if we were anywhere near the harbour. I didn't ask Errol. I preferred to wait and see. I eventually realised we were moving inland. Iconic Sydney was far behind. There was nothing ahead but a thick suburban fringe.

"It's a full house for this weekend's retreat," Errol said. "Jimmy's retreats are always popular."

We finally took a turn up a road, past a final cluster of houses, and then along a stretch lined with eucalypts and scrubby bush. I could see rolling green hills on the right and flatter paddocks on the left. Errol drove up a long, curving drive past a spacious and well-trimmed lawn. There was a large building, or group of conjoined buildings, up ahead.

"That's the retreat centre," he announced. "But with all the rooms occupied you will be up at the cottage."

We drove around the back of the building past a double-storey wing that Errol said was the retreatants' accommodation. I looked out, to the left, at a broad panorama of rolling paddocks. I could see cattle on a nearby hill and a battered old ute rattling over the grass towards them. There was a hint of suburbia along the lower fringe of the property, but it was otherwise a rural setting.

There was an old timber house behind the main buildings. I imagined it was the original farmhouse. It sat just above a tall, triangular building. I guessed that was the chapel. Errol took my bag and lead me up a cracked concrete path to the timber house.

"Hi," said a familiar voice. Chris came into the

hall.

"You're in this room." He pointed to a small bedroom just to the left of the front door. "I'm in the corner bedroom, and Michael is in the other room. Michael's the vicar general. He's the head of the order in Australia. Now you're joining the retreat, aren't you?"

I nodded.

"Good. There's a talk on shortly. I will show you down to the conference room when it's time. In the meantime, settle in. Make yourself at home. There's a kitchen up here with tea and coffee, but not much more. The main meal is lunch. You will be eating with the community down in the main building. That will be directly after Jimmy's talk. Let me know if you need anything."

"Hallo there," chimed in another voice.

An older friar emerged from the far room. He was wearing the tunic of the habit unbuttoned at the top.

"I hear you've just flown in from the mainland," he said, and flashed a broad smile.

I laughed at his reversal of the standard vernacular distinguishing Tasmania from the rest of Australia. The man clearly knew the way to a Tasmanian's heart.

"Well, you're welcome here," he added. He wandered back to his room with a chuckle. I could hear him melodiously mumbling to himself with a Donegal cadence.

I put my bags down in the room where I was staying. It was a small room. There was just enough space for a bed and an old-fashioned wardrobe. I looked out the window and could see the triangular end of the chapel just beyond a large tree. There was a covered walkway, further down, between the far end of the chapel and the main building which was down on the right. I could see a timber building to the left of the chapel. It had the look of a large kit home. I found out later that it was the novitiate building.

CHAPTER NINETEEN

The lecture room was full. The people on retreat were mostly middle-aged women. Some had pens and paper on their laps ready to take note of any striking word or phrase: a quiet, poignant something to ponder in the noise of their ordinary lives. Others sat with their eyes closed, waiting for a personal epiphany: a delicate annunciation best received lightly and left to settle deeper than the mind can hold.

Some friars were sitting at the very back, near a wide opening to another room. It was a packed room of quiet people. Waiting. There was a palpable feeling of expectation. God was somewhere in the wings waiting to enter centre stage.

The room itself had seen better days. There was an old piano next to a side door, a largely empty bookcase along a brick wall with a token number of dog-eared books focused on spiritual topics, a sad plastic plant display, and a Gospel-themed wall-hanging that looked like a sorry remnant from the 1970s. Windows looked over the front of the property and towards the chapel. Morning sunlight beamed through the room from the side windows.

Jimmy was sitting behind a table at the front of the group. He was quiet for a time and then looked around the room as though surprised to discover he was not alone. "Are we all here?" There were nods from retreatants eager to get on with the business at hand. He got up and came around from behind the table and stood before the group. His woolly grey hair and crumpled habit gave an immediate sense that this was a man from some prophetic fringe.

He started quietly with a prayer. "Come Holy Spirit, fill the hearts of your faithful and kindle in them the fire of your love. Send forth your spirit and they shall be created, and you shall renew the face of the earth."

Tried-and-true retreatants knew the appropriate responses. Others remained silent. The intercession of saints was invoked in a business-like manner and then the prayer finished.

He paused long enough for silence to return and then began to lay out a scene: an oceanic place before creation, inchoate, formless, deep and dark – the fluid element of an ancient cosmology. He laid it out and let his words hang in the air, so we saw and felt the water and knew our share in it: chaos waiting to be deciphered, the dark before a solid world's declared.

Jimmy lingered and teased out the implications of an ancient language. The words weren't so much pondered but plucked with an outstretched hand, broken into portions of possible meaning, tasted and offered. He spoke an ancient phrase to the room, *ruach elohim* – the spirit of God, but also a great and powerful wind, an elemental breath that stirs the waters. Jimmy conjured the biblical drama of creation. It unfolded as an elemental dance: the great wind breath spirit moving, brooding across dark, primal waters. Power meeting the undefined, stirring over it, separating and dividing, making firmament, form, shape, sense.

I sat in the middle of the conference room, in that tight-packed room full of people, but they all fell away. There was just this woolly-headed man in front of me, in his bedraggled habit, and with his Irish voice rising and falling like the waters he was calling into the room. Every time his eyes met mine, I felt a tremor inside myself. All the chaos I had spent a lifetime trying to hold back was present in me. It was conjured by the story he was telling. It pressed to crack my feeble attempt to contain it, and tears started streaming down my face. I couldn't stop them. I didn't want to. *Ruach elohim.* Couldn't I feel creation working in me? Wasn't this why I came to Sydney, to meet the power that would give me shape, decipher truth out of my chaos, make me someone new?

I wasn't the only one with tears. They rolled down the cheeks of nearby people. Noses trumpeted a loosening of emotions. Jimmy's eyes briefly met mine, but they didn't register shock or embarrassment. This was the work he did: telling stories, striking truth. Jimmy held and drew everyone in pursuit of this chaotic water as it seeped and gushed through biblical narrative. He planted us in a crowd of slaves pressed against the barrier of water, where nothing was possible but the chaos of a drowning death or further captivity for generations to come. And liberation wasn't planned. It was pure gift: a solid way forward through the waters. He drew us into the muscular struggle of Jacob wrestling a stranger in dark waters. The waters that must be crossed. A blessing that must be given. Necessity birthing contention. Jacob grasped and refused to let go, even to the point of dislocation. The waters gushed all around – the whole business raw and elemental.

The room was filled with the struggle, tenacious and desperate, holding tight because a thing must be achieved. And the stranger was a man in Genesis but, in Hosea, an angel. And after the struggle was done, a struggle that was a brute experience of something that might be faith, the stranger gives Jacob a new name that means 'contends with God'. So, Jacob becomes Israel.

Each story revealed spiritual life as an immersive human drama: an elemental dance, a tenacious battle, a necessary contention, a drive to truth that must be pursued and gained through the experience of life.

Jimmy drew the room from these ancient stories to the newer ones, the Jesus stories, and there was the water again. John the Baptist in the middle of the Jordan River, and Jesus insisting that he should be immersed in the water because that water, the rolling chaos that's yet to gain its form, the element of life and death, is not something to escape. It's the element where truth will be made known. And then we were at the pool at Bethesda whose waters were sometimes stirred by an angel and offered healing, but now that elemental work was superseded by Jesus' command. Rise, take up your bed and walk. And then we were with the woman at the well, hearing a promise of living water.

Finally, the waters subsided. Jimmy drew it all to a conclusion with a reminder that lunch wasn't far off, and then there were some hours when people were free and very welcome to wander the property, as long as they remembered to close the gates behind them.

I continued sitting in the conference room as it emptied. I felt exhausted. There were waves of emotion rolling around inside me. I ached to have the privacy to curl up on a bed and surrender to it until I was done sobbing. I went back to the cottage and laid down in my room for a while. I had about half an hour before I had to face the community. I felt I was in the worst possible state to go and meet a community of Carmelite friars.

CHAPTER TWENTY

The friars' dining room was full of men when I arrived. I was self-conscious. I had been crying and I presumed my face was a mess. I hoped it wasn't too obvious. I wondered how I could make any kind of good impression given the state I was in.

"So, you were at the retreat talk?" asked Michael.

"It was powerful," I replied. "I've never heard anything like it."

"Yes, he does have that effect. It's why we hate him so," the old man joked.

The dining room was a dingy place. There was one small window, at the end, that let in a feeble amount of light, but the space was mainly lit by fluorescent lights above. A long table, with chairs, ran through the middle of the room. There was a serving hatch at the side where trays of food were passed through from an industrial-sized kitchen. There was a small fridge beside the hatch and a sink between the fridge and the window. The trays of food were placed on a side serving table along the opposite wall. There was a meat-and-vegetable casserole on offer and rice.

It was a small space for an apparently large community. I looked around and counted nine men. Some were in habits and some weren't. I knew some of the men already: Jimmy, Chris, Michael and Errol. I lined up for food and then sat beside a bald old man. He had a lively face and smiled at me and said I was very welcome. Most of the men seemed quite old apart from Errol and Chris and another man in a habit who looked Indian.

"What's your surname then?" asked a beanpole of a man who had the scraggy grey beard and energy of an Old Testament prophet.

"It's Donnelly," I replied.

"Irish then," he declared.

"My ancestors came out as convicts," I added.

"Not convicts," replied the beanpole, "they were patriots, Robert."

There was a rousing cheer from fellow Irishmen, as the beanpole looked at me with a quirky smile. I felt a moment's pride and connection, but it soon dissipated. There were too many people in the room. I didn't know how to find my way into the conversation or whether I should say anything. What did these men expect of me? How was I supposed to be? The community and my doubts all crowded in as I forked food into my mouth.

The bald man beside me lent over to me, introduced himself as JV, and tried engaging me in conversation. He had an Australian accent, though I later found out he was yet another Kiwi.

"Have you been to any movies lately?" he asked.

"Yes," I managed to say.

"What did you see?"

I looked at him. My mind was completely blank. "I can't remember."

The old man laughed and shook his head. I laughed too. I was lost in this strange new world. I was lost inside my own head and the intensity of what I was going through. My mind was still washed through with the tumultuous waters of scripture, and I was sitting in a humid little box of a room where men were dressed in habits designed centuries ago, and they were engaging in conversations that suggested we were in nothing less than a little Ireland that had accidentally fallen into South Western Sydney.

"Well, if it isn't the late PP!" Michael boomed as another old friar meandered into the room.

The new arrival pulled off his beanie, scratched his head, and wandered over to the side table to dish out his lunch. He peered down at the content of the trays and expressed a quavering consternation.

"Where's the potatoes?" he asked no-one in particular.

An ancient man with the head of an old bull, sitting at the end of the table, mumbled a sympathetic noise as the newcomer sighed, dished out his unsatisfactory lunch, and then took a seat opposite me. He looked across at me.

"Hallo. You must be Robert," he said. "I'm Paddy."

His face had soft traces of melancholy, though his eyes shone with an occasional delight at a comment made by one of his Irish confreres. He was content to sit and listen to the booming to-and-fro of the performers at the table. Jimmy peppered the conversation with humorous anecdotes. Terry, the beanpole, seemed to enjoy playing devil's advocate to presumptions that he heard in other people's comments. The old Irishmen were deep-rooted in their country of birth. They spoke about vigorous games of hurling, played in their adolescent years in the juniorate of the order, as though it happened only yesterday, and they still had the cuts and bruises to prove their vigour. The superior qualities of one county over another were called up and debated by these men. The debate came to a head in consideration of who would win the All-Ireland in the year to come.

The ancient man at the head of the table sat chewing his food and half listening to the back and forth of the conversation. He occasionally mumbled something that could hardly be deciphered in the communal noise. When he wanted to be heard, he interjected with a more forceful "I say" which he repeated a few times until the others stopped and listened. There was no Irishman in the room who had been in Australia longer than old Brother Kieran. He had seen it all. He had walked the back streets of post-war Manila begging money to build a church. He had taken the generous donations of pious Filipino hookers and been chased by their gun-toting pimps. And he had been in the group of founders who came to Australia to start a monastery of Discalced Carmelite friars.

Paddy asked me to stay on after lunch, so we could have a talk. The friars wandered off after they had finished lunch. Some went into the kitchen to clean the dishes. Others wandered away to their rooms for an afternoon siesta.

"So, I suppose you have been told that I am going to be the novice master for the upcoming novitiate," Paddy said.

"Yes. Chris mentioned it to me. He said you are also the parish priest."

"Yes," he said and sighed. "This is the life. We go where we are called to go and put our shoulders to the plough."

I nodded.

"Do you know – a friend of the community from up the road was down the other day laying the concrete path over to the novitiate? There are crosses in the path. I wonder if one of those crosses might be for you?"

"Maybe," I replied nervously. "I'm certainly praying to try and find out what God wants from me."

"Well, you know the novitiate will be happening probably the middle of the year. It would be a good thing if you might come to a decision. Maybe during this visit."

"I will try."

The conversation left me raw. There was a timeframe. My indecision was clearly a problem. Who knows when another novitiate might occur? It felt like it was now or never. I wandered across the walkway to the chapel to pray. I told myself I wouldn't leave until I had an answer. God's answer. Surely it would come. I sat in a pew and looked towards the tabernacle directly behind the stone altar. A large cross was framed by a triangle of clear glass that looked out on a tree. Its branches and leaves were dancing in an afternoon breeze. The great water theme was still rolling around in my mind. My head throbbed with the pressure of it. Now was my time to stand in the river, struggle, contend, demand an answer. I had to grab and hold on until the answer came, even if it left me dislocated. Even if it left me close to drowning. It had to come now. I had to know now. I had to have a definite decision to take to the old Irishman.

My mind brooded over everything that had happened in less than two years. I thought of the nights when I hammered out poetry on my old typewriter, peered out the window at the sleeping world of Hobart, and found my way to Gethsemane. I thought of my cousin the nun, my bewildering visit and the conversation through bars, the question about the priesthood. But then I thought of my years of resistance. How often had I thought there was nothing so stupid as a lifetime of celibacy? How often had I wondered whether the church's ways had anything much to do with your ways?

This was my struggle. It was primal and instinctive. It carried the weight of all my life. I grabbed, twisted, slid, near drowned in all the contentious currents inside my soul. My life. Your will. I cradled my head in my arms and started crying, but there was no way that I was moving from that chapel until I had an answer. I remembered those moments, the feeling of being grasped, the inexplicable tears, the murmuring of Teresa through her writings, the sense of a deep living connection. I remembered the student master in Melbourne, casually sitting in the midst of all his books, and the way I felt when I talked to him. There was too much in my head. There was too much in my heart. I begged you to show me what I should do. I begged from the midst of the storm inside me. And there was just one moment. A sweet spot of stillness.

The peaceful centre of the storm. It was there and I knew the answer. I knew the thing I had to do.

I walked down the road to the parish church which was just a community hall. Paddy was busy at his desk, so I waited. I studied a map of Ireland that he had up on his wall. He eventually came over and spoke about his hometown, Killaloe, that sat beside the River Shannon. I told him I had grown up beside a river too. I told him I was ready to say yes and join the order. I was told to go home to Hobart, pack my bags, and get to Melbourne as soon as I could. I was to commence studies immediately. The start of the new semester at the theological college was only a few days away.

CHAPTER TWENTY-ONE

So, my destiny was ultimately worked out over a handful of days in early 1990. One day I was a confused twenty-two-year-old with an engineering degree, living in Tasmania and clambering to find solid ground where I could build a convincing future. The next day, I was a postulant in a catholic contemplative religious order in Melbourne. The ultimate turnaround from one state of life to the next involved little more than a quick flight to Sydney, an overwhelming preached retreat, a fever-pitched decision, a quick set of marching orders, then a one-way ticket from Hobart to Melbourne.

It had been a quick but fierce birth. My whole family came to see me off. My brother-in-law was particularly excited by the occasion. He boomed a great farewell and kept peppering encouraging comments through the air, as I joined the queue to be processed and board. He had always brought that kind of energy to family occasions and made up for the quiet reserve of his in-law family members. Mum saw me off with tears in her eyes. Dad was the same, but with a measure of restraint. It was a peculiar turn of events for most of the family, but they were as supportive as they could be.

The presence of my family exacerbated something inside me. I had no idea when or if I would return. The departure was not just a messy birth. It was the swift application of a blade to the umbilical cord that connected me to the only world I knew. There was a darkness about it. My every step across the tarmac said I want a life, so I have to leave this place. I can't find my life here. I need to leave. I must. What was there for me if I stayed? Maybe a job with the Hydro Electric Commission – at best, designing stormwater drains or some other mediocre trifle, and even then, I'd be constantly wondering how long they would take to discover I was a fraud. My effect on the material world would be wrought with failure and embarrassment would surely follow. I couldn't bear such a precarious life. I had known too much of it already.

I wanted truth. My instincts said it was bound up in an act of surrender, and I had been feeling the possibility of it: in the Carmelite world and in the audacity of Teresa who showed how to let go and be given over to the greater life. I wanted to be a saint like that. It wasn't a thing to admit. Not to anybody. Not yet. I wanted that pure leap of spiritual surrender.

But this snotty, tear-soaked limp across the Hobart tarmac was the reality of my surrender. My heart was an anchor resisting every step, as I hunted in my pockets for a serviceable tissue. I didn't want to leave. I wanted to stay. I wanted to turn around and get in a car, walk back into my home, into my room and into my safe world of dreaming great dreams that were always better than anything life was likely to really offer. And yet my feet kept moving forward, because they knew my old dreams were spent and there was nothing left to be found there.

In that moment, walking up the metal stairs and

into the plane, I knew that birth and death are one. My tears spoke of death. Finding my seat, sandwiched between two people, and fastening my seatbelt for departure were the practical preparations for birth. My mind was addled by these contradictory currents, but my body seemed to know what it was doing. It knew how to navigate the rapids of dying and being born. It declared truth through both tears of grief and a settling sense of relief. It wrote excitement on my face, as the plane accelerated and lifted off the ground. It expressed overwhelm as my fingers struggled to open the small milk container for my coffee during the flight. The woman, next to me, offered to help. She probably presumed I was on my way to some final death-bed farewell or a funeral. Why else would a grown man occasionally sob on a flight from Hobart to Melbourne? She would never have guessed I was on my way to start a new life in a monastery.

PART TWO

CHAPTER TWENTY-TWO

I walked into my assigned room with the bags I had packed in Hobart. I put them down on the bed. I was on the top floor of the two-storey accommodation wing in the Discalced Carmelite student house in Melbourne. The room was brighter than the one I stayed in downstairs when I previously visited. There was a large window in the centre of the wall opposite me. It looked past the red tiled roof of the adjacent chapel and across the road to a small grassy park and a neighbouring apartment block.

I arrived as a postulant. I was no longer a visitor or an aspirant. I had a probationary status, but that categorical change didn't alter my appearance. I didn't have the regulation-issue brown habit. That would be given in a clothing ceremony to mark the beginning of my year as a novice in Sydney. I hadn't taken vows. First vows were taken at the end of the novitiate year and renewed every twelve months after that, until final lifelong vows were taken towards the end of studies. If things went pear-shaped, as a postulant, I could leave or be told to leave without a moment's hesitation.

Postulancy did involve living in the monastery full time and learning the ropes of monastic life. That meant full participation in the daily rhythm of prayer and worship, carrying out weekly assigned duties that included cleaning the communal bathrooms, vacuuming floors, setting up the chapel for mass and other liturgies, grocery shopping and taking a turn cooking the evening meal for the community. It also meant completing a semester of theological studies at the neighbouring college. So, I went straight from finishing a four-year engineering degree to starting a new one. No time off for good behaviour.

There was a sound of water, surging and splashing, below the window. Ryan was standing in a courtyard casually watering a herb garden. He was oblivious to my presence above, as he stooped to investigate something in the bushes. The scent of assorted mints, basil, thyme and rosemary merged and drifted up to my open window. I doubt I could have imagined a more monastic scene. Ryan could have been a medieval apothecary tending to his herbal resources, and yet this scene was in the middle of suburban Melbourne in 1990.

I felt a possibility as I stood there with the sunlight spilling through the window, listening to the sound of water and breathing in the scent of herbs drifting from below. This was now my space in the world and only the second home I had experienced in my life. This was where my new life might mingle with the ancient currents of a religious tradition and find its true shape. My destiny was waiting in the cloistered seclusion of this room and in the austere space of the central chapel with its white-washed walls and old choir chairs. It would come to me through countless morning masses and the chanting of psalms and the quiet of two hours meditation every day. This was where I might finally surrender to the primitive spirit of Carmel: a deep, bewildering inclination of the soul to be alone with some cavernous something that calls from within.

I wondered how long it would take to fully surrender to that ancient spirit. It had been around long before the dark days of the Inquisition and Teresa's reform movement. The first Carmelites felt the spirit as they followed the bloody tide of crusaders and the blasphemous brutality of a holy war. It seized their souls and sent them clambering up a rocky mountainside in Haifa to find caves where they could be alone. Their individual stories are unknown. Maybe they were crusaders appalled by their own brutality or atrocities that they had seen carried out in the name of God – hard men brought to face their darkness and pray in search of mercy and hope. Maybe they were pilgrims who found everything they sought in the lonely recesses of rocky hills and valleys.

The cave was each man's solitude. It was bare and cold and right. It could hold a fevered memory, a thread of revelation, a sullen bout of midday devil lethargy. There was space to live and die and live again in a rhythm hidden from the world. The mountain that the first men shared held them as community: a strange band of brothers together in their solitude. They were there before any rule was written, before any name was given, before any ecclesiastical sense was applied to what they were doing. They were there simply because they had to be. The necessity was deeper than words could reach. Its pull had the nature of gravity.

The first men were on Mount Carmel. Geography eventually gave them their name. And the local church authority, Albert the Patriarch of Jerusalem, eventually gave them a rule, at the beginning of the thirteenth century, largely based on his observation of what the men were already doing. In his words, they were hermits called to take up places in solitary areas where they were to pray and meditate on the law of the Lord, by day and by night.

That was the beginning. A long history of dislocation and adaptation followed. Then there was Teresa with her pen and her back-to-basics revolution. The whole history was threaded with the vigorous presence of that ancient spirit.

The Melbourne student house was built on that primitive foundation. But it looked to the future as much as to the past. It was an extraordinary act to build a generous house of religious formation in the late 1980s. The bricks of its two storeys of accommodation were laid when the general catholic religious landscape was contracting due to dwindling recruits. The old ways were dying. The old structures seemed to be crumbling. Parishes were amalgamating due to the declining number of parish priests. This decline was already in play before the darkest truths of the church were exposed. But the Discalced Carmelites laid down an architecture of hope, close to the theological college and the small community houses of other orders, with trust that its steady stream of vocations would continue.

CHAPTER TWENTY-THREE

It was late afternoon and the monastery echoed with the sound of methodical violence. It was repeated, time and again, homicidally vigorous, breaking the silence. I wandered down the stairs and into the kitchen. Sam was striking through the flesh and bones of a raw chicken with a meat cleaver. There was no delicacy about the business, and there was an intensity about him. His eyebrows had converged in a knot. There was a trace of sweat on his forehead. I could have sworn this was about more than chicken. Down went the cleaver again.

He noticed me standing at the door, and the intensity melted into a smile. He sniffed, pushed his glasses back into place with a finger, and raised a portion of the brutalised meat.

"We're having Chinese KFC tonight," he said, "with some other Chinese dishes. Do you know how to use chop sticks?"

I signalled my uncertainty with a wiggle of my hand. He chortled. "Well, you'll soon learn brother."

There was an intense fishy smell about the place, and I could see a strange assortment of green vegetables, that I didn't recognise, along with an oddly elongated cabbage. There were bottles of ingredients labelled in Chinese. They seemed to be quite ancient. There was a fully loaded rice cooker bubbling on a side bench, an intense red sausage or cabana that was chopped into pieces in a dish, and a packet of shrivelled dried mushrooms that had partly spilled on the table.

"We have a good Asian supermarket up the road," Sam said. "I'll show you. Maybe tomorrow? Have you settled in? You're upstairs aren't you, right over the top of me, I hope you don't snore?"

"Yes, I've settled in. Thanks. And no, I don't think I snore."

"Are you looking forward to starting studies?"

"I think so."

He brought the meat cleaver down again. The impacted bone fragmented into shards, but this seemed to be of no consequence to Sam who was keen to continue talking. "What subjects are you enrolled in?"

"Introduction to Theology, Church History, Philosophy."

"Ah. You'll have Max Charlesworth. That's good. He's a significant Australian philosopher like your Eric D'Arcy."

"Oh," I said, not knowing what to make of my apparent possessive claim on the Archbishop of Tasmania. "And I have a scripture course."

"Good, good. They like Carmelites over at the college. They see us as different from the other clerical orders. We're contemplatives. People like that. They like the idea of meditation and our saints."

"That's good," I replied.

A heavy-set man then came into the kitchen.

"Ah, Father Walter. Have you met our new postulant, Rob," Sam said.

The priest gave me a darting glance, mumbled g'day, and then directed his attention back to Sam.

"I won't be in for dinner," he muttered.

"No worries," said Sam.

The priest made a quick exit and paced along the hall, out into the courtyard, and up the stairs past the chapel door.

"So now you've met Finch," Sam said. "My advice is, keep your head down when he's around and stay on his good side."

"Errol in Sydney gave me pretty much the same advice," I replied.

"Really. What did he say?"

"That Finch can make your life hell on earth if he doesn't like you."

"Yes, well, Errol's talking from his own experience. He was here in Melbourne studying, but there were clashes. He ended up moving to Sydney without finishing his studies. It's awful when Finch decides he doesn't like someone in community. I've seen him go for months completely freezing a student out, as though they didn't exist at all. He won't say a word to them. Not even 'pass the salt' at dinner. And a lot of the time you're completely in the dark about why he's doing it. It could be anything. Just some innocent comment, but there he is with his nose out of joint. You could go mad trying to work it out."

"How can it be avoided?"

"Well, the best you can do is avoid antagonising him," Sam said, as he slammed the cleaver down on the chicken one more time for luck.

I made a cup of tea and went back upstairs to my room. I wondered what to make of Finch. I didn't know whether it was the things I had heard about him, or my own instinct having seen him, but I suspected I'd have to keep my radar on when he was around. The monastery apparently wasn't exempted from that core lesson I learned from my early days of school: whenever two or more males are gathered there's always a likelihood one is an unpredictable bastard, savage as a dog, so you best keep your guard up just in case. And if you can't identify him in the group, then it's all the more necessary to be ready, because it could be anyone.

One trip down to the kitchen was enough to shake my vision of my divine-union-bound contemplative future. I was in a monastery with two priests in charge. One was a strangely compelling, semi-cipherable mystic devoted to his herbs. The other seemed to be a cantankerous bastard bordering on something worse.

I tried to reassure myself that there was some sanity and ordinary humanity in the place. Sam was friendly and sane, though his vigour with a meat cleaver was rather disturbing. He was certainly the most socially engaging person in the place. My fellow postulant Julian was friendly. Checkers was quick as a flash, in and out of his room with an athletic devotion to the hidden life of Carmel, but I suspected, from my brief encounters, that he had a good heart. I hadn't spent any time with the other two postulants. I knew one was a Croatian from Sydney who was about my age. He had arrived about the same time I did. The other was an older man from South Africa.

CHAPTER TWENTY-FOUR

The doors of the college lecture rooms opened onto a classic cloister. Its sheltered walkways bordered an enclosed garden: a patch of green grass racked by the shadow of a lovely tree, a space for a stirring breeze of fresh air and dappled things, a flourish of nature befitting a surrounding Franciscan-built establishment.

There were still Franciscans in residence under the same roof but beyond the college walls. There were two old Franciscan priests with expertise in ancient languages and biblical exegesis, who lectured at the college, and there was a group of brothers who ran a printing press. The sizeable building had once been riddled with young men studying to become priests in the spirit of Saint Francis of Assisi. That time was long past. The landscape of cities and towns across Australia was dotted with the re-purposed shells of a once-triumphant church: convents turned to art galleries; churches now boutique bars; monasteries transformed into ready-to-book conference centres.

The relatively new Discalced Carmelite student house was on the same block as the college. It was only a couple of hundred metres to get from home to class and back again along the tree-lined driveway to the carpark and the back entrance. There were other religious communities gathered nearby: Divine Word Missionaries, Redemptorists, members of the Blessed Sacrament Congregation. Small communities of religious brothers and nuns lived in suburban houses around Box Hill and Blackburn, while others travelled from farther afield. The Dominicans had a large community and a prominent church in Camberwell.

I wasn't sure what to expect the first time I gathered up my pens and paper, raced down the stairs, and joined the other postulants in the short walk to the initial Introduction to Theology class. A brief glance at the college's enclosed garden suggested peace. The impression briefly lingered as I entered a room full of people: male and female members of religious orders and congregations and a mixture of lay people of varying ages. There was a quiet tension about the place, a kind of non-verbal white noise, a sense of positioning, traces of people making new beginnings or taking new stands, quiet assessing glances around the class, cynical whispered asides.

The lecturer was a nun whose manner betrayed her past history as a no-nonsense schoolteacher. I imagine she might have once ruled the world of kids with the striking command of a well-gripped ruler that bruised more than its share of knuckles. The crisp lines of a former religious habit had given way to a soft silk blouse and a sensible dress, but the old-school inclinations of her past bristled as she endeavoured to plot a course through the complex currents thrown up by the students in the room.

"So, what is faith? How would you define faith, Ivan?" she asked.

"Well, Margaret, Saint Paul would suggest faith is the substance of that which we hope for, the assurance of things that we cannot see."

Ivan's words were a sonorous lasso sailing through the air towards his intended target.

The nun melted, just a fraction, at the sound of her name. How long had it been since someone had proffered it so tenderly? She liked the new Carmelite postulant despite herself. His manner ensured she would direct questions to him throughout the semester, and he would always answer with a Cheshire-cat smile and the intonation of an indulgent parent.

"Very good, Ivan," replied Margaret. "So we have Saint Paul's definition and we might come back to that later. What about the experience of faith in our own lives, in our particular experience? How might we define it in that context? Yes, in the front."

"It's the thing that keeps you going when everything's falling apart."

"Good. So, in some sense it's something that moves us, a certain strength that sometimes seems to stand in contradiction to other aspects of our lives. How does faith relate to the church?"

"Sometimes it's there despite the church."

There was an immediate hum of sympathetic agreement at the front of the class and a bristling discomfort among clerical students at the back.

"Well, I don't have faith in a church that won't ordain women."

"Hear hear!"

"Here we go," Julian, who was sitting next to me, vigorously murmured in my ear.

A thousand and one raw nerve endings began to fire inside me as the class continued. I wasn't ready for contention and forming sides, allies and enemies, battlelines and verbal skirmishes, and all the theological tinnitus of the modern church. I wasn't ready for the pain and friction of contradictory truths: the truth of the middle-aged woman in the front of the class who was finally throwing off the belief that father knows best and was fiercely looking to find herself and speak her mind; the truth of the early-twenties clerical student trying to find his way towards a life of service, grappling with the impending sacrifice of celibacy, and looking to assert the importance of the priesthood in a situation that felt like it was being disparaged; the truth of the pious young woman, in the corner, with a heart racing to bring love and healing to the pain that she could hear in the voices around her; the truth of the Aboriginal student sifting blessing from curse in the religion that had clashed against her ancient culture.

The room was full of abundant truths – soothing, surging, contending and clashing – a reactionary stew of emotions, a flurry of stories reduced to sharp shards. I hunkered down, like my old schoolboy self, hoping not to be noticed. My life had radically changed in the space of days. I had no idea what I was doing, but I was sure it wouldn't be found fighting these battles. But those personal truths, the anger and tension, the faces that flashed with vulnerability and pride and frustration – all came into me despite my efforts to withdraw. I absorbed it all, because that's what I do, and it felt like holding broken glass tight. It cut deep and it was only the beginning.

In the end, Margaret reined in the conversation

and brought the class to a conclusion with the suggestion that what we had just experienced could be rightly named church – not a church of uniformity but diversity; not a church that owned the truth, but a pilgrim group on a journey towards truth.

CHAPTER TWENTY-FIVE

It was obvious when Finch was having a good day. He wandered the student house as though walking the backstreets of a Joycean Dublin. Then he was none other than Buck Mulligan, a roving finesser of words and dispenser of ribald asides, hunting the monastery crevices for the local equivalent of a Stephen Dedalus.

I was in the kitchen talking to Julian when Finch wandered in humming a jolly ditty that sounded vaguely Irish. He was an entirely different man from the sullen, scowling creature I had first encountered. His eyes settled on Julian and narrowed with reptilian delight. Finch had found his Kinch.

"Well, there he is," Finch exclaimed, "the answer to a maiden's prayer. What gourmet extravagance is on the menu tonight, me auld segotia?"

Finch was not Irish, though he had spent some years studying in Dublin and living in Irish communities. He was Australian born and a convert to catholicism. So was Ryan whose origins were equally unexotic. He was originally from suburban Adelaide.

Julian blushed in response to Finch's attention. He momentarily clenched his cheekbones, forced a smile, then answered.

"Roast lamb and vegies, Father Walter."

"Hmm," said Finch, with leering delight. "A touch of your old mother country Julsie Woolsie! Well, you can count me in."

Sam arrived at that moment. He half stepped into the kitchen, quickly glanced around, mumbled that he had stupidly forgotten something in his room, lightly hammered his forehead with his fist as though to emphasise the point, and then turned and went back up the stairs into the accommodation wing. Sam's comic execution of the fundamental monastic skill of avoidance left a lot to be desired.

"There's one you have to watch," Finch the prior said. "Old Uncle Sammy. He's as cunning as a shithouse rat that one. But I'm not telling you anything you don't know already, am I Julsie?"

Julian responded with a grimacing smile that was hard to decipher. He was tense and possibly angry, but he kept it contained. Postulancy wasn't a time to be getting on the wrong side of superiors.

"There it is," Finch said, as he pointed at Julian's face and laughed. "Aye. Old Julsie Woolsie's got the lowdown on Uncle Sam. Ah, but discretion's the better part of valour isn't it, young fella me lad? That'll be three Hail Marys right there and bless your cotton socks!"

Finch took up the chorus of his ditty and wandered out of the kitchen satisfied his formative interaction with the postulants was done for the day. Julian raised his eyebrows at me and shook his head with disdain.

"He really is quite mad," I said.

"Shh!" replied Julian. "He might hear you."

We came down for dinner after chanting evening prayer and an hour's private meditation. We queued to serve ourselves the lamb, roast potato and assorted other vegetables. I was hungry and looked forward to an old-fashioned roast. Ryan took his customary position at the head of the table and Finch was to his right. I was sitting further down beside Sam. Julian was opposite. The prior's good spirits had not abated.

"Ryan and I had Paddy as our novice master. Did you know that?" Finch asked.

"No," murmured Ivan, who was sitting opposite Finch, "and what was he like?"

"Hard but fair," Finch said, while chewing a chunk of meat. "I'd say that. Of course, he thought the sun shone out of Ryan's arse. Didn't he?"

Ryan smirked and shrugged his shoulders.

"You should have seen this fella as a novice," Finch continued with a nod towards Ryan. "Kneeling at attention to Jesus he was. Hours on end. Pious to the point of bursitis. That put an end to your spiritual long march, didn't it, when the old knees gave out."

"And yet here I am," Ryan airily countered.

"Anyway," continued Finch who was on a roll, "Paddy will be alright. Hard but fair. Hey, remember that scrawny piece of work Johnnie in the novitiate?" he asked Ryan. "He had a mouth on him that one. I gave him a right walloping out the back paddock. Remember?"

Ryan shrugged and kept eating.

"Really?" Ivan asked with unrestrained delight. "What happened after that?"

"He was sore and sorry. I can tell you that. And Paddy was all aquiver and suss that something happened. Nothing came of it. Anyway, Johnnie left soon after, but not on account of that."

He speared another piece of lamb with his fork,

then waved it emphatically at Ivan.

"The thing is novitiate is an intense time. Grace is in facing what comes to the surface. This fella next to me thinking he could stormtroop his way to Jesus on his knees and then coming a cropper. That bursitis was grace. Right. The failure was grace. Intentions don't get you far. If you think they do, then you're in for a hell of a surprise. The spiritual life's struggle and failure, dissatisfaction, being prized open in a state of utter need.

"That's the starting point. It's not communing with whatever fluffy, pious phantasms you lot currently have floating around in your heads. That isn't the spiritual life. That's delusion. That's what that is."

I quietly cut my lamb and scooped a generous amount of gravy on it. The roast potatoes were just about perfect. Crunchy on the outside and fluffy on the inside, just like a good pious phantasm. I smiled, but kept my joke to myself.

I looked across at Finch and didn't know what to make of the man. Was he a mad bastard I should never trust or was he a rough-as-guts fount of spiritual wisdom? Maybe he was both. Maybe he was a real-life version of Graham Greene's whisky priest: a morally dubious character saved from his worst instincts by the great good that grabs and uses him despite himself. Maybe that was the spiritual life: grace making good out of what's mad and broken.

CHAPTER TWENTY-SIX

It was Saturday. We were free to take off and do our own thing once morning prayer, community mass and the morning hour of meditation were done. The great city of Melbourne was full of possibilities for Ivan, Julian and me. We were brother postulants, all in our early twenties, and facing the strange monastic adventure together. On that first Saturday, we couldn't wait to get out of the monastery, find the normal world and let off some steam. Hansie, the South African postulant, was happy doing his own thing, free from the presence of the mere boys who he looked upon with a bemused incredulity.

We managed to claim the student van for the day, so we were free to go anywhere, and as postulants, we were still free to access our money, so there were no financial constraints. I was glad Ivan claimed the role of driver. Julian didn't have a licence, and I felt nervous about driving in a big city. Ivan sat behind the wheel with his smooth self-assurance.

"Right, first things first bloody," he declared as he turned the ignition. He fingered the buttons of the radio, found Midnight Oil singing 'Blue Sky Mine', and turned it up to near maximum volume. He reversed out of the garage and took to the road with Julian yelling directions. We cruised through Box Hill and down the tree-canopied stretch of Mont Albert Road, singing along as Peter Garrett smashed out his protest lyrics against a world of big business and working-class vulnerability.

We made a quick left, then right, and found ourselves on Barkers Road. The towering cluster of the city centre was ahead. It was a long way from the unchanging world of Hobart where I had grown up. Ivan floored the accelerator. I gave a walloping yell of joy. It was as though a button had been pressed and my nature was unmuted. Tension fell away and I was sitting in the back seat filled with an unfamiliar delight.

"Where are we going, Jules?" asked Ivan.

"Carlton," said Julian the navigator. "Let's go and get something to eat, and then we can work out a plan."

Barkers Road turned into Victoria Road, over the Yarra, and straight into the heartland of inner suburban Melbourne. Richmond. Collingwood. Carlton. All the familiar names rang in my head and a great bustling intensity was all around: a shopfront fusion of ethnicities, endless cafes, a cracked tiled pub on a street corner, a barman hosing away the detritus of the night before, golden arches, hospital signs, a group of girls with neon-coloured tops, short shorts and cowboy boots – more than a glance and the ache might become too much. Public housing towers cast desolate shadows over streetscapes of graffiti and dust and the clanging presence of green and orange trams. Druggies and homeless dudes clustered around shadowy stairs; old ladies were bound for the markets with their pull-along shopping bags.

I drank in the earthy glory of it all. It was good: a great mad symphony of good. Yet the monastery chapel and its quiet, the solitude and the murmuring of the ancients, and the praying were good too. I was alive in both places. Was it the same life or two separate lives? Life in the monastery. Life in the world. Did one have to be suppressed so the other might grow to the full? Did my truth and destiny really require a sacrifice of one vital side of my nature for the sake of the other?

I put my thoughts aside. They were too heavy, too impossible, beyond solving. It was Saturday, and I was happy, and surely that was enough for now.

We found a park and walked through the Queen Victoria Market. Italians and Greeks were competitively booming out their prices for grapes and bananas, apples and pears. "You won't find a better offer in the market. Prices to go. Do yourself a favour. Come and take it off my hands. Look at this. Lady finger bananas half price now. Come on over. You don't need to go anywhere else. The best fruit and veg in Melbourne right here. Don't bother with the rest. Come and buy the best."

It was hard to believe Ivan could become more expansive, but the joyous cacophony of European accents provoked him into an amplified state of something he described as unmitigated wog pride. He walked past the produce with his shoulders back and his chest out, in his superman T-shirt and jeans, a somewhat corpulent bristle-faced superhero, nodding at an Italian here and a Greek there, all near neighbours to his great Croatian homeland and all brimful of Mediterranean vitality.

I hadn't been sure of Ivan until that day. We had sat at the feet of Ryan, the student master, in the monastery earlier in the week to puzzle our way through John of the Cross's poetry and prose book, *The Spiritual Canticle*. Ivan was quick to establish his credentials as a Sydney University philosophy graduate. He referenced Aristotle and the saint philosopher, Thomas Aquinas, with a confidence that I found unnerving. He pushed the conversation into technical considerations of terms used by John of the Cross. It felt like the metaphysical equivalent of a class in engineering analysis. The soul seemed reduced to a nuts-and-bolts thing. I didn't like it at all. I preferred the flow of the conversation when the ancient poem and prose sparked associations from the world of our own experiences. The world of stories was my natural domain. There was no better feeling than coming out with an insight and seeing Ryan's eyes spark with a pleasure because I had managed to say such a thing. It was like pleasing God himself.

I came to see Ivan differently as I walked through the markets with him. He might have been a smart-arse, but he was full of life and made me laugh like nobody else, and that counted for a hell of a lot. We wandered around for a while, drank coffee and settled on a kebab for lunch.

"Let's have a drink," Ivan said.

We found a shadowy tavern under the old Southern Cross Hotel on Bourke Street, ordered pints all around and a couple of bags of chips, then found a booth. Julian ripped the bags open, so the chips fell in a pile in the middle of the table. The place had a video jukebox. Sinead O'Connor was on the screen, near bald and gorgeous, singing her desperate sad new song. The one Prince had written. We quietly sat, sipping our beer, and looked up at her as she looked out from the screen. Her eyes had an enveloping power. Vulnerable. Passionate. Beseeching. Tears rolled down her cheeks. The glory of a woman like that. The glory of being loved that much. It was enough to make us all sit quietly for a while.

"Life without sex," Ivan eventually sighed.

"Yeah," I replied.

"I suppose we've got time before making the ultimate decision," he said.

"I don't know about that," Julian said. "I mean, you're either committed or not. That's what I think."

There was an awkward silence. The beer eventually helped loosen things up again, and then the Red Hot Chili Peppers came on the screen singing 'Higher Ground'. Ivan started drumming the table with passion. This was followed by a round of impersonations of Finch and Ryan. Then Ivan shared his experience of the toxic challenge of cleaning the downstairs monastery toilets, which he shared with Finch, Sam and Checkers.

We spilled out of the tavern and wandered through the city. It was dark, and we knew we had to return to the monastery. Any regret was brushed aside. It was only a week until next Saturday.

CHAPTER TWENTY-SEVEN

It was clear to me, from the beginning, that monastic life found its pulse through a regular encounter with the word. There was The Word: the Messiah, the Saviour, the Son of God, the Alpha and Omega, the scrubby Prophet of Middle Eastern appearance, the Ground Zero of christian religious consideration and intent. But traces of that Word gleamed in an endless rolling ocean of text that was laid down and cobbled together over centuries, then taken up and prayed for centuries more.

The community's job was to pray these words. Every catholic monastery and congregation around the world was praying the same words and pondering the same passages each day. So the global church, through these commonly prayed words, was bound in a journey together through liturgical seasons every year: waiting for a Saviour; seeing a Saviour born; sharing the Saviour's mission; watching him die; witnessing his resurrection from death; feeling the outward push of the Spirit into the world to share an extraordinary new life.

It should have been easy to stand up and read out loud. I was an educated twenty-two-year-old man. I was highly literate. There were no issues with dyslexia or anything of a similar nature. But things went wrong one night, in the early days of postulancy, when I had to stand and read a long passage to the community at a time in the daily liturgy called the Office of Readings. I could feel trouble looming before I got up from my seat and walked across to the spindly lectern in the middle of the chapel. My heart was already racing, despite my deep breaths and my increasingly urgent prayers. I felt a catastrophic wave was moving at a great rate of knots towards me. It sent me spiralling back to another time.

I was gathered with my schoolmates on a bright summer afternoon twelve years earlier. We had to demonstrate to teachers that we could swim by crossing the breadth of the Hobart Olympic Pool. I knew I could swim for as long as I could hold my breath. I reached the front of the line, pushed aside my uncertainty with a bravado that surprised me, and dived in. I was fine for as long as I held my breath. I almost made it all the way across, but then I noticed how deep the water was, and I was gripped by a vertiginous fear.

I needed to breathe, and I couldn't. I clamoured to seize hold of anything and almost grabbed the foot of the kid swimming ahead of me. The solid world was slipping away. I couldn't find the surface. I struck out with all the fury in my body, completely disoriented, and took water into my lungs. I started sinking. It was just a moment, but enough to feel the claim of the deep. I was hauled out by a lifeguard and laid at the side of the pool convulsively coughing. It was the first time I felt the proximity of death.

I revisited that moment when I was a postulant in the chapel that night. I stood, walked to the lectern, and looked down at the page. The words in my breviary became an impossible ocean. I had to get across. My heart started accelerating. My chest and throat tightened. My breath lost its conviction. My tongue was a dry thing set to undo me with every word. My skin became cold as death, yet strangely clammy. I felt the eyes of the community on me, noticing my struggle to breathe, my stumbling over the simplest words, my utter humiliation. Their attention crashed down on me like dreadful waves. I was drowning, pummelled by watchful eyes, betrayed by my erratic body and filled with anxious shame.

I was most conscious of the two priests when the panic attack seized me. I looked up, and there was Finch fiercely communing with his god of tension and catastrophe now made manifest in the tremulous presence of a postulant. And there was Ryan, exuding the well-cultivated calm that was his yin to Finch's yang, but nevertheless noticing the moment in what he would call "all its particularity".

I spilled out of the chapel and was thankful of the cool night air. I could breathe again. I was still alive. My cheeks were red with shame. I wanted to cry, but knew I couldn't. Tears would be the end of me. I retreated to my room as quickly as I could. There was a knock on my door about an hour afterwards. Ryan came in.

"So, ah … there was clearly something going on for you during tonight's office. Some distress possibly?" he asked.

"Yes. A bout of nerves. Sorry about that."

"Yes. Um. There can be some significance in a thing like that. Walter has certainly expressed some concern to me. Now, ah … there is a psychiatrist who has very good standing with ourselves and other religious. A good man. Highly qualified of course. I wonder if you would be open to maybe having a chat with him?"

"Sure."

"Good. I've had a preliminary conversation with him. He indicated it would be most appropriate for you to ring and book the appointment. Maybe you could call tomorrow morning?"

"OK."

"And well, certainly I am here. There may be wider considerations that might come from this in terms of discernment that might be worthwhile for us to have a conversation about."

"OK. That sounds good."

"Walter and I know about this arrangement. Nobody else in the community needs to know unless you choose to share it."

"Fine."

"Good. Well, I will leave you the phone number."

"Great."

Ryan left. I turned and looked out my window into the dark. It had been far from a warmly empathetic conversation. It was more like organising to get a problematic car serviced. I wondered what the two priests had said in their conversation about me. It was a relief that they hadn't simply arrived at a conclusion that the panic attacks were a clear sign that I didn't belong in the monastery. I was safe for now.

I didn't hesitate in agreeing to see a psychiatrist. I trusted Ryan and I wanted a solution to the panic attacks. I didn't want to go through that again. It was awful and humiliating. Apart from all that, I was intrigued where a psychiatric process might lead. I had never been to a psychiatrist or psychologist. The closest I had come to that world was reading self-help books and my copy of Jung's *Selected Writings*. Maybe this was a good thing. Maybe it would help me understand the deeper reasons behind my choices. Maybe there was some kind of grace in this panic-ridden moment of failure.

Finch stopped me in the hall the next morning. I was startled. It was the first time he had stopped to directly engage me in a conversation. Most of the time I had just been a spectator to his interactions with others, particularly his auld segotia Julian.

"Have you rung yet?" he asked me. His face loomed with the fiery tension of a Japanese Kabuki mask.

"No. I'm going to though. Definitely."

"You should," he almost spat the declaration. "Look, he's a bloody good psychiatrist. He used to be a religious. He was the superior of his order before he left, for Christ's sake. So, he knows exactly what all this is about ... the life, the stress, right. There's no shame in it. This is what the life's about. Understand? I've been to him. You don't see me moping around with my tail between my legs, do you? He's good at what he does."

"That sounds good."

"We wouldn't send you to some wack job, if that's what you're thinking. You think we'd send you off to some wanker in a kaftan with fucking incense sticks and bullshit?"

"No. I'm sure you wouldn't."

"Well, fucking ring him."

"I will."

Ryan drove me to my first appointment with the psychiatrist. It was a crisp autumn afternoon in Melbourne. Everything was vivid to my eyes: blue sky above, still air, sunlight spilling over suburbia. I was heading down the road towards a therapeutic resolution to my problems. Classical music was playing on the radio. Ryan was relaxed as he drove along the well-to-do streets of Camberwell. Conversation was minimal.

"After this first meeting, I think you can drive yourself."

"Sure."

The psychiatrist had his office in his home. He was an older man and he greeted me with an air of professional indifference. He was so much the part that he wore a black turtleneck skivvy and his office walls featured totemic artefacts. I went into the first meeting with the intention of confessing all that had ever troubled me: family difficulties when I was growing up, my relationship with my parents and siblings, my journey into religious life, my social struggles, my feelings of inadequacy. I had read my share of Jung and thought I knew the drill. I blurted out all the broken pieces of my life with an unquestioning trust that the psychiatrist was going to help me piece it all together. Why else would the priests have sent me to him?

I spoke until I ran out of words and anticipated that he would focus on some interesting point in my personal revelation and start the process of talk therapy. I was ready for a long therapeutic journey into my psychological wilderness. I braced myself for the likely appearance of Oedipus and Narcissus. I knew I was a mumma's boy through and through. Surely that was significant.

I looked at him. He silently sat, eyes caste down, scribbling notes. I waited. He scribbled. I thought of something else to say. I spoke. I ran out of words again. He scribbled some more.

Surely this appointment was about helping me face and work through my issues. That's why I had agreed to come. He scribbled more notes. My words collapsed into an awkward silence. Maybe this was part of the deal. Me digging deep and nothing more than that. The first appointment ended. I had said as much as I could, and he had written pages of notes for no obvious therapeutic reason. Nothing helpful had occurred. Maybe the helpful stuff would happen next time.

I went back to him once or twice more, and then he called an end to the sessions. He managed to pause his dedicated note taking for just long enough to comment that the panic attacks were driven by a fight-or-flight reaction and that my body would eventually grow tired of generating the drama. He provided no insight into the cause of the attacks. It didn't seem to be a matter of particular interest to him. He made one observation that I thought was quite odd coming from a psychiatrist. He suggested that I probably had a vocation, at least for the present time. I came away from his fine Camberwell house with no greater understanding about why I was going through my drama. The panic attacks continued for another eighteen months.

I was sitting in the monastery lounge room. It was the day after the last session. Finch saw me through the open door and came in.

"See, it all went well, didn't it? You weren't put on any medication. What did you think? Did you think he was going to have you drugged up to your eyeballs mooching around the monastery like a fucking zombie?"

Finch entered the lounge room with his arms raised like a zombie: Bela Lugosi in monastic drag. He collapsed in the chair beside me.

"Well, he said you don't have to be on anything, and even if he did, it's nothing. I'm on medication. What do you think? You think I'm a fucking zombie?"

I had no idea what to say to him. I looked at this bizarre man who had a leading role in my formation to become a priest, and I felt a surge of rage. I could barely contain it, but I knew I had to try. In that moment, I understood what the psychiatric sessions had been about. They weren't about helping me work through whatever issues had led to my panic attacks. They weren't about helping me understand what drove my choices, shaped my motivations, and inhibited my growth. The sessions were about observing me. The single-minded focus on note taking was the preliminary step towards making a report. The outcome of the sessions was a matter between the psychiatrist and the priests. I had been observed and assessed, and I was left in the dark regarding the nature of those observations.

I had kept the appointments to myself at the time, and not mentioned anything about it to the other postulants. I told them some time later. Julian said he was sorry I had gone through it alone. He was irate that I had been assessed without knowing it, and that there was a report about me that I hadn't been shown. He said I should demand to see it. His feelings were stronger than mine. As far as he was concerned, this was evidence the order couldn't be trusted.

I just wanted to put the whole business behind me. At the time I thought I could. The psychiatrist's failure to help me, and the ongoing experience of the panic attacks led me to spiritualise my distress. The attacks were a weakness, possibly like Saint Paul's experience of his fleshly weakness, so I was obviously experiencing the trial so that I would rely on and trust grace alone. The more my body trembled with anxiety, the more I prayed. The more my psyche shook my body with its need to be heard, the more I focused on the weak and dying Jesus on his cross. I took to repeating the line "when I am weak then I am strong" whenever the time to get up and read was approaching. I even went so far as to try and befriend the symptoms of my panic attacks. I would welcome them as old friends as they appeared: the accelerating heartbeat, the tightening chest, the desperate shallow breathing, the cold and clammy dread. Surely they were all propelling my utterly weak and needful self more deeply into the arms of God.

CHAPTER TWENTY-EIGHT

I was sitting at my desk reading one evening when Julian burst into my room. I was taken by surprise. There was no knock. There was anger in his eyes. His teeth were clenched. His jawline flexed with a now familiar bony tension. I stayed at my desk as he loomed over me and braced for whatever was coming.

"You have to go tonight! It's not fair that you get to stay home while the rest of us have to go," he erupted.

It took me a moment to work out what he was talking about. The postulants had been invited to the Redemptorist student house. I had only heard about the invitation second-hand and hadn't committed to going. The Redemptorists lived just up the road in a suburban house. Their priests were away, and there was a full liquor cabinet. I suspected the night would involve a combination of booze and cynical despair, an evening of frustrated testosterone and bitching. The thought of going was surprisingly unappealing to me.

"Nobody has to go," I said.

"Of course we do. They invited us. It's the right thing to do. Don't you think I'd rather be back here? How's it going to look if you don't come?"

I was shocked by his rage. It had the coercive intensity that I had come to associate with Finch. I didn't know what was going to happen next. Everything in his bearing suggested physical aggression. I tensed, ready to duck a flying fist, ready to push back if he should grab me. I struggled to stay calm as adrenaline coursed through my veins. He was taller than me. There was no doubt about that. Maybe I had more speed. Maybe.

My adrenaline hinted at a rage I might summon if needed. It was thundering through my body, fuelled by everything I had been going through: the pointless appointments with the psychiatrist; the leering prior; the exhausting grind of panic attacks; the steadily accruing sense of shame and failure; the demanding complexities and contentions in the college; the monastic cell-bound scurrying in a place that was questionably called a community; the difficulty of knowing who to trust in a place that was meant to be about God. There was enough rage inside me to fire up an army but I didn't want any of it. I was sure rage would destroy me.

But still, I had been doing what a Carmelite was meant to do that night. Sitting in my room, in my cell, pondering scripture and praying. And apart from all that I thought Julian was my friend. Yet there he was, mad as the maddest bastard in the monastery, and for what? A sad piss-up with a bunch of other students for the priesthood who I barely knew and had no great interest in getting to know.

I stuck to my guns and insisted that I wasn't going. He switched from rage to pleading, made some suggestion that it was good for young members of religious orders to connect, and then threw out the unlikely suggestion that it might be fun. I repeated that I wasn't going, and he eventually left. It was my first intimation that life in the monastery, and particularly my friendship with Julian, wasn't going to be plain sailing.

I did go one other time, to avoid another bout of Julian's outrage. I had already started telling myself that I would pick my battles with him. One of the Redemptorist students was leaving the order. The night was exactly as I anticipated. There was a considerable amount of drinking, and then we all looked through a book of old photos.

It developed into a strange game. Spot the priest who's still in the order. We possibly knocked back a drink whenever we found one. Fingers stabbed at the photos. "He's left and he's left and he's left and he's left." It went on for page after page. One face after another, groups of newly ordained priests from the 1960s through to the 1980s, hope in their eyes, a lifetime of mission and service ahead of them, young men just like us, ordained and then gone. Sometimes the holy oil of ordination was barely dry on their hands before they were out the door. Sometimes they were in ministry for decades before they left. Sometimes they came out of the closet. Sometimes they came out straight. One way or the other, they certainly came out of the priesthood.

At the heart of it all, in the midst of the photos and the pointing, the drinking and cynical asides, there were dark, lingering questions. What the hell were we all doing, entering the dying world of religious life? What were we doing journeying towards priesthood when the church seemed at war with itself, when we were seen by some as new recruits to the problematic patriarchy, when the value of mandatory celibacy was increasingly under question, when the hope of simple loving service seemed lost in the endless battle between conservatives and liberals? What were we doing diving into such a crumbling world?

The questions waited on the edge where the liquor ran out and the hangovers began. They remained, like a little stone in a shoe, as we went about our daily routines, gathering in the chapel for morning prayer, going to college for classes. The questions were there in the shadows and around the corners, in the moment a pretty girl passed by, in a class assigned text for discussion that challenged the authority of the church. Would we stay or would we go? What was the future of this strange life we had just entered? The questions never went away. They gained weight as time went on. We spent our days suspended in the gravity between contending answers.

CHAPTER TWENTY-NINE

Postulancy took us from the summer of 1990 through to its winter. The six months had delivered an extraordinary concentration of experiences: transitioning from an ordinary suburban life into the foreign world of a monastery; negotiating the strange range of personalities in the community; trying to find an orientation in the contentious battleground of the theological college; experiencing the increasing maul of anxiety, the vertiginous dread of panic, and the underwhelming assistance of a psychiatrist; feeling the joy of mateship and the pleasures of youthful adventures in a big city; sifting the grains of trust and belonging and many questions that remained unanswered.

We relocated to Sydney in preparation for the year-long novitiate. It was due to begin with the clothing ceremony, which involved being literally clothed in the habit of the order. Our variety of Carmelites was discalced, meaning shoeless, so sandals were required for the ceremony. Ivan was determined to buy a fine pair. I think he was after something that had a classic Roman look. He decided the most likely place to find such an item was Oxford Street. Julian and I went with him, and we were soon searching through stores that featured an exotic constellation of leatherwear, but not a satisfactory pair of sandals.

"Are you boys getting ready for Mardi Gras?" asked one shop assistant.

"Something like that!" Ivan replied with a smile

PART THREE

CHAPTER THIRTY

The novitiate building stood beside the friars' cemetery on the retreat house property in Sydney. It was the kind of timber building that people use for a shack or a cheap holiday house on a bush block. It was hot in summer and too far from the coast for the consolation of an evening sea breeze. It was cold in winter, but the worst chill was driven away by a pot-belly stove, in the middle of the lounge room, that glowed red hot at night. The bedrooms, or cells, were on either side of a long hall that reverberated when anyone walked down it. The kitchen was at one end of the hall. It was mainly used for breakfast. The novices ate their other meals with the main community. The room at the other end of the hall was used for the novices' morning lessons.

The property was rural but bordered by the urban sprawl of Sydney. The sounds that filtered into the building were from a mixture of country and suburban worlds. The community's cattle bellowed when the calves were sent to market and the mother cows stampeded across the hills in their frenzied, tear-soaked grief. Kieran, the old brother in the community, was often heard bellowing at the livestock as he rattled around the hills in his old ute. Hoons roared up the adjacent road, mainly on Friday and Saturday nights, and it was no surprise to see the burnt-out shell of a stolen car at the top end of the road the following day.

The novitiate was there to house us for the year, directly after we had been given the Carmelite habit.

It was an intensive year living the monastic life without the distraction of going off to college or any other outside activities. It was a time when the novice discerned his vocation and the community considered his suitability.

The novice master and his assistant lived in the novitiate with the novices. The rest of the community lived in the retreat centre and the old farm cottage. At times during the year, the community gathered to consider the novices and vote whether they should stay or go. This happened behind closed doors. The novices could do nothing but pray and wait to hear if they had been voted out. In some ways, it was an ancient forerunner to a reality television premise. In our season of novitiate, there was an all-seeing God, a predominantly Irish community, an assistant novice master with liturgical ambitions and an old beanie wearing novice master from County Clare called Paddy.

The clothing ceremony occurred in a late afternoon in July 1990. The sun was going down as I lined up with Ivan, Julian and Hansie. We stood in front of the altar. The soft-spoken Irishman Michael, who was the head of the order in Australia, entered from the side. The chapel was empty apart from the gathered friars and my parents who had flown from Hobart to witness the event. They were proud but had made a point of telling me I was assured of their love and support whether things worked out in the novitiate or not.

The large Sydney community, who I had first encountered six months before, were gathered in the choir section behind the altar. All the old and young men, the Irish, Australians, Kiwis and others, were there to witness the beginning of a new novitiate. They wore the flowing white mantles of the order. They hung cape-like from their shoulders down over the brown habit and added a sense of majesty and formality to the occasion. A new novitiate was no small thing in the life of a religious order.

I was nervous of course. I quietly hoped that I wouldn't disintegrate into some panic-ridden heap at a crucial moment of the ceremony. I looked at Michael. There was a weary kindness about the man, and an inclination to go about the process in an understated, murmuring manner. He was simply doing the thing that needed to be done that afternoon. There was something reassuring about his manner.

I could feel the neatly folded habit in my arms. I held it in my outstretched arms like the other postulants. Prayers were said, then Michael introduced some vigour with the holy water. It splattered over the habits we held, and more than one dollop hit and ran down my face.

The tunic was the first item to go on. I put it over my head, head through the unbuttoned hole, arms through the long sleeves. It was essentially a baggy, long brown dress that unfurled down to my ankles. My body was lost underneath it. Mine was secondhand and a slightly paler brown than the others. Julian's was new and cut to measure on account of his height. Ivan looked like a sausage bursting at the seams.

In the midst of the strange sight of four men putting on brown dresses, reference was made to putting on the new man. Each item had a story and we were taken into that story as we put the habit on. The cincture, a store-bought leather belt, fastened around the tunic at the waist. It was symbol of girding the loins for the sake of chastity but also being led down the path that God intended. The scapular, a long rectangle of brown cloth with a hole cut out for the head, hung at the front and back as a symbol of taking on the yoke of obedience and also being in relationship with Mary, the mother of Jesus. The capuche, a brown hood, carried a sense of the hidden life as well as putting on the helmet of salvation. The mantel was a long white cape with a hood. It was the most dramatic element in the habit. It swirled and could fly out at the back, in a superheroic manner, when there was a gust of wind. In the order it was a sign of purity and was worn for significant liturgies.

I progressively put on the habit with the prayers and symbolism ringing in my ears, until I was fully clothed as a Carmelite novice. The four of us stood and looked at each other in our brown habits and the dramatic white of the mantel. We were dressed the same as the rest of the community who now filed down to greet us with a hug and best wishes for the year ahead.

This strange baggy clothing from another era was a sign of brotherhood. It stirred a fire of aspiration in me. I wanted to belong. I wanted to grow old wearing that habit, living a life of prayer, finding my place in a religious community. I wanted to take up the baton of that ancient life with its traditions and spirituality and take it forward into the future. I wanted to live and die in the order, surrendered to God alone, and I intended to endure any trials that came in order to achieve that goal.

CHAPTER THIRTY-ONE

My best intentions leading into the novitiate soon clashed with the complications of my mind. I was sure from the beginning of the novitiate that my novice master, Paddy, didn't like me. On the rare occasions when I opened my mouth to speak when he was around, I saw his face contract into a grimace. It was as though my voice was the sound of nails on a blackboard. His forehead tightened into a braille statement of anxiety. His eyes contracted into slits of distress. The sound of me clearly caused him excruciating pain.

Once I saw that grimace, I shut up. My throat tightened as a bolt of panic charged through me. I had been stupid to speak in the first instance. I broke one of my basic lifelong rules of survival. I made myself noticeable and therefore vulnerable. Now the beanie-clad angel of death was right in front of me. If I said anymore, he would hear the shredded sound of my anxiety. His grimace would firm into a resolution, and then he would invite me to his room for a quiet little chat to tell me that I had to leave.

A large portion of my novitiate was that mental war played out in my mind every day. It was a war between me and that grimacing face and everything I associated with it. I was alone on that frontline. The other novices weren't like me. Julian and Ivan were so self-assured they joked around with the old man as though he didn't have the power of life or death over them. Julian would come out with a humorous comment and Paddy's face would transform into a look of wide-eyed wonder that then broke into a smile. That smile looked like a pure and unrestrained, bright-eyed Irish validation to me. *Julian's such a nice boy. We'll keep him. He belongs.* Then Paddy's eyes would turn to me, and it was as though the smile had never been there. Instead there was anxiety collapsing into complete despair.

I told myself your kind and benevolent will was the ultimate power in charge of the situation. If you wanted me in the order, then I would be there no matter how much the old man grimaced. But my peace-seeking spiritual reasoning didn't make much difference. My nature was wired too deeply with the lessons from my past. I looked at Paddy, and all I could see was the shadow of the fatherland.

It was 1979. There was evil in the daylight hours of school: the threat of the strap in the shadows of the Crying Room, the malicious intent of my grade-six teacher, the cancerous uncertainties of life. They swirled and coalesced in the dark. They crept over me when I was in bed on a school night. They fingered a chill desperation through my twelve-year-old veins. Everyone in the house settled into bed and drifted asleep. I shuddered with the loneliness of my predicament. I was stuck awake on a solitary star in a vast, sleeping universe.

I needed safety. I looked for you. I lay in the dark with my good shepherd holy card in my hand. My eyes fixed on it as though it might be a doorway to a safe universe. Maybe my world wasn't right because my belief was too weak. I gazed at the good shepherd, the flowing robes, the lamb on his shoulder, the benevolent smile. I held the picture in my mind for as long as I could. Surely holding was believing. Yet tomorrow was always there, in the shadows, and none of my prayers could hold it back.

I packed and repacked my schoolbag before going to bed. I repeatedly checked that I had done all the homework and the extra work assigned to boys whose names were listed on the board for punishment. I was a hypervigilant mouse at school. I kept my head down and my mouth shut. The safest thing to be was nothing at all. My name was rarely listed on the board. But I always did the extra work each night, just in case my name was there and I didn't see it. How could I be sure of my senses? Maybe my eyes lied. Maybe I missed hearing some final direction. How could I be sure of myself at all? It was safer to cover every contingency in the face of all that uncertainty.

Every night Mum piled my neatly folded school clothes on a chair beside my bed. I believed the next day would be OK as long as that pile stayed exactly as Mum arranged it. There was safety in the order, the clear folded edges, the overall arrangement. The pile was a sign that school was at a temporary safe distance: the clothes were there in undisturbed stillness. They were there so there was still time before the day began and the clothes would be unfolded and the uniform put on. There was still time before getting on the bus or getting a lift with Dad, crossing the river, ascending the hill, lining up for assembly, being inspected for shined shoes and gartered socks, entering the classroom, shrinking to nothing. There was also time to think, to dread, to imagine the worst. Sometimes sleep brought me something other than consolation.

I was alone in my bedroom at the back of the house. It was dark and quiet. The blinds were drawn. It was just another night at home. Suddenly there was an explosion, shards of glass flying through the room. An enormous male lion landed in the middle of the chaos, shook shards from its great mane, stretched its limbs, drew its lips back to reveal its lethal teeth. The lion reared its mighty head, opened its mouth, and let out a bloodcurdling roar. It sent sound waves through my body. Then it saw me. I looked into its eyes. There was nothing but darkness: a tense, muscular hunger made to maul and shake a kid like me into a thousand shreds of flesh.

My body flooded with adrenaline, my bowels twisted into a knot, my heart pounded with rib-breaking intensity. I was charged for fight or flight, but unable to get to the door or move. I was unable to fight against the enormity of the threat. I was fixed to the ground. The king of beasts crouched, wound up like a spring, a low growl reverberated through the room declaring lethal intent. It was ready to launch at me. I tensed tight as a spring. I roared with utter fear. I woke up yelling and grasped the edge of wakefulness. I swallowed the lion back into my dark.

Dad drove me to school the next morning. The red-brick institution sat squat on top of the hill above Hobart. It was a Christian Brothers' school built on the old catholic cemetery and made to propel scrubber catholic boys into a professional ascendency. I was overwhelmed with fear and panic as he stopped outside the school gate.

"Please Dad, please, don't make me go. I don't want to go. I can't. Please."

I begged and pleaded, tear soaked, clinging as though my life depended on it, hoping he wouldn't make me get out of the safety of the car. I'd declared the dark horror inside me. It was my one desperate bid to be heard. He looked at me. He grimaced.

"Well, I have to go to work and you have to go to school and that's all there is to it," he sighed with his deep-grained melancholy.

There was no malevolence in it, and it wasn't for want of sympathy. It was just the only reality he knew. The day always demanded its pound of flesh. What was there to do but pay the price? What else was there to expect from life? Pain was inevitable. The one consolation was not to let the bastards know you're hurting. Don't make a song and dance about it. Settle down. Simmer down. Hold it in. Grin and bear it. Offer it up. It will be over soon enough.

There was nothing more I could do. I got out of the car, stumbled up the stairs, and looked back to see him drive down the hill to his work. My fear was a salt-stained, snot-green ugliness. It was an embarrassment and an inconvenience. It was the foolishness of a weak child. The tremulous start of a story best smothered before told. I had to bury it. I had to deny it. I had to show myself to the world as something other than it. This was the legacy from father to son handed down at the front gate of the school: male virtue as a cross-bearing endurance that has to stay one step ahead of the treacherous weakness of the heart. This was the legacy that is the fatherland.

I am twelve years old at the top of the stairs of my school. My father's driven down the road to his unhappy job. I'm trying to hide my tears before anybody else sees how wrong I am. It's bad enough that I showed my father. It was the last act of hope for a safe world. I should never let him see it again. I am twenty-three years old and a novice in a religious order. I'm immersed in a world of fathers. The old men watch. They gather, behind closed doors, to vote on my suitability: black-and-white marbles into black-and-white boxes. Black into black and white into white is yes. Black into white and white into black is no. I already know the lesson for a place like this. I learned it a long time ago. I can't let them see how wrong I am, how my soul sometimes falls into fragments, how I absorb so much I think I might explode, how often I am lost in the world. The panic attacks betray me, but I can contain that chaos. I'm already well-practised from postulancy. I will be the quiet novice. I will pray and you might come this time. Maybe. Finally. A good shepherd who's more than just a consoling picture. The other novices can do the talking: Ivan with his charm and humour; Julian with his youth and earnestness; Hansie with his age and certainties. If I become nothing, I might survive. If I hide myself enough, then I might belong.

CHAPTER THIRTY-TWO

The kitchen walls of the novitiate squeezed tight when we arrived after mass and morning prayer. It was an awkward space. The simple business of getting breakfast was a negotiation around other men's bodies and eccentricities. I sat staring at a round of toast thinking this is what religious life is all about: discovering myself dressed in medieval attire and in the company of strange men I would probably never cross paths with in any other circumstances. Yet here I was, stuck in the awkward intimacy of religious brotherhood – the whole scene so unlikely and outrageous, it could surely only be attributed to the will of an unfathomable god.

Julian was busy in the kitchen. He now believed he could push through novitiate powered by his exacting religious devotion and the continual appeasement of his considerable appetite. He hovered over the stove top in the morning, boiling water, then cracking and poaching eggs with a single-minded military precision. I was occasionally caught up in his enterprise and cajoled into a state of readiness.

"Come on Rob, where's the toast? The eggs are ready," he invariably snapped. Everything had to be just right, timed to perfection: buttered toast on the plates ready to receive the eggs with their yolks runny but not too much. Everything in its right place. Everything carried out in a right order. Religious rubrics grafted to a culinary enterprise. Chris, who was wrapped in a custom-designed woollen brown mantel to keep himself warm, had no great interest in eggs, but he had a brittle concern regarding the state of his toast. "It has to be cool and dry otherwise it's utterly unpalatable," he said as he arranged his two lightly browned rounds in a kind of teepee for cooling and drying purposes.

Hansie had taken to eating his breakfast standing, as this was apparently an old custom in the order. He hovered, demonstrating his newly acquired verve to quickly eat then get on with the day, while Ivan slumped at the end of the table in a state which may have been an extension of his hour-long, semi-comatose meditation in the chapel.

Paddy sat opposite me and looked around at the activity with a kind of meek wonder.

"Are those eggs you're making, Julian?" he asked.

"They certainly are, Father," Julian replied with a tense smirk. "Would you like some?"

"Well, if it's no bother, yes I suppose I would."

Paddy looked across at me for the first time that morning. His eyebrows raised in amazement at the good fortune that had befallen him.

"Julian's making me eggs, Rab," he said, with his customary strangulation of my name.

I nodded with an unconvincing smile. How else could I respond? I continued staring at my toast, knowing in a few minutes I would be on the solitary side of my room's closed door. There, I would indulge my current fantasy about leaving the Carmelites and joining the Camaldolese hermits in some obscure European mountaintop monastery. There I could be alone, rapt in an unsullied state of lifelong contemplation, without the jarring complication of communal interactions and the ever-present threat of Paddy's grimace.

Communal interactions complicated everything. They even complicated my feelings about Paddy. There was no monotone chanting of the psalms during community prayer in Sydney. The old friars were inclined to a simpler execution of the spiritual work. The psalms were therefore read in a natural style with the usual antiphonal dynamic of one side reciting one stanza and the other side responding with the next.

Paddy's voice stood out from the others when the psalms took on a melancholic theme. This was particularly the case during night prayer. Then he channelled all the feeling he could muster into the lines, with his voice surging and moaning in travail, begging God not to forget his promises or abandon his people. His body lent into the words. His eyes peered up and his hand rubbed back and forth on the top of his thigh in rhythm with the recitation. He was so given over to the business that every cell in him was caught in this act of beseeching: a beanie-clad spokesman for a broken world.

In those moments, the old man found a home in me, despite myself, and left me with a crowded contentious heart. Nothing was clear. Nothing was easy. There was beauty and truth and bullshit in the life. There was tenderness and there was judgement. There was an antiquated structure that named old men masters and put young men in the dock to be judged. There were ancient, broken words waiting to be brought to life and they were often as paradoxical as the men who came to speak them. It was all a dark bright ocean far from any solid world, and I wanted a solid world. Yet there was only this, and I was as likely to drown in my love of it as in my disdain for it, and as novitiate progressed, I was vulnerable to the whole of it.

CHAPTER THIRTY-THREE

Chris sat in the end room of the novitiate. He had a pile of books on the table in front of him, as he faced his four novice charges. It was time to put a bit of stick about and get us thinking outside the box of our limiting pieties and the lingering influence of any delusional hagiographies we might put stock in.

"Let's get started," he said. "We have Our Holy Mother, Teresa of Jesus, founder, reformer, a woman with a vision, a woman of her times. The question I want us to consider, that we all need to consider, is what does it mean to be authentically Carmelite in our times?"

"Being truly faithful to her vision of the life," Julian promptly offered.

"Be specific, define your times," replied Chris.

"Saint Teresa's vision of this life was simple enough," Julian said. "It was about prayer and, specifically, the two hours of mental prayer, meditation, daily community mass and the recitation of the divine office."

"So, adhering to a structured prayer life: is that the extent of what's required for us to be authentically Carmelite in our times?"

"Living in community," Julian continued, "and living in a way that's true to what's specified in our constitution and, more broadly, what the church asks of us."

"Adherence to both a structured prayer life and constitutional requirements. Is that all there is?"

"There's the experience of charism," I offered.

"Yes. More," Chris prompted.

"There's that experience of a personal connection with Saint Teresa," I replied. "Her words matter in a personal way. Being here is about that. It's about living out the reality of that relationship, sharing in her vision and mission through that relationship."

"Anyone else?" Chris asked, as he looked around the table.

"Well, yes," Julian jumped in. "There is that personal sense of charism. The caution is, that can be such a subjective thing. That's why we need the guidance of the church which speaks with the voice of God and gives us a clear and unifying direction."

Chris gave a slight sigh.

"Let's reframe the conversation," Chris said. "When we think about being authentically Carmelite in our time, at this point in history, does that mean living in a way that's as close as possible to the structure, look and conditions of the first reforming Carmelites' lives in sixteenth-century Spain?"

"That's absurd," Julian charged in. "I mean, obviously there are things about the way we live today that just weren't available then. We use cars and that sort of thing. But there's a connection between having a clear and visible continuity in the way we live our religious life and the quality of our witness. I mean look at us. We're all in habits, aren't we? The same habit that Saint John of the Cross wore, and that continuity makes the connection and our identity clear to the rest of the church and the world."

"And yet you're discalced," Chris countered, "but you're wearing those appalling, grubby shoes. Haven't you compromised the continuity putting on those shoes?"

"I'm not saying there's not a place for adaptation. The church says as much."

"So, adaptation is OK," Chris said, "any adaptation?"

"Within the bounds of what's allowed in our constitution and the broader teaching and direction of the church," Julian replied.

"What about the nuns?" Chris asked. "We're right in the middle of a lot of discussion about their constitution. The grille, the iron bars in the parlours, is a hot topic. Is the fidelity of the nuns all about recreating the way of life and conditions of Teresa's first reformed Carmel in sixteenth-century Avila? Is fidelity, being authentically Carmelite in our times, about recreating something from the sixteenth century?"

"No," said Hansie, "authenticity is surely about being true to the spirit of Carmel, the spirit that led Teresa to her life of prayer, in the context of today's world. We need to be open to the times. We need to be informed by the times. We're not sixteenth-century friars. We're men living at the end of the twentieth century."

"Yes, but that whole language of being true to the spirit is so often a cop out," Julian retorted. "How many orders are around today who say they're being true to their founding saint's spirit, but you wouldn't even know they were religious, looking at the lives they're living. There's no visibility. There's no witness. Usually there's little community and no prayer.

They're just odd, eccentric men who happen to live under the same roof. It's no wonder those orders are dying out. Nobody can see anything that's worth joining."

"But I put it to you, Julian," Chris said with a concluding tone, "that a life that's lived as though time and history is irrelevant is a life that makes a god out of unyielding structures. That's something worse than a cop out. That's idolatory."

Every conflict-averse fibre of my being was tense as I listened to the two young men. The exchange was civil, but with a brittle edge on both sides. I knew Julian would come looking for me later to debrief about the class. He'd be wound up and aggravated and all the more so if he thought I was being nonpartisan. God help us all. What would I say? They both made strong points. I was a long way from settling on a clear position about what should be conserved and adapted in religious life, but deep down, I leaned towards Chris's take on things.

Change and adaptation were inevitable. They were inevitable in the order's ancient times. They were inevitable in the present. The contemplative world of Carmelites had long been susceptible to waves of change. The first wave was centuries ago. The original men of the mountain had passed away, but all the while, religious warriors continued locking horns down on the Palestinian plains. They raged with their zealous self-righteousness and bloodlust. And it was all for the Lord Jesus Christ and Christendom or for Allah and the growing Islamic Empire.

The men of Mount Carmel watched from their

rocky height. They were distant, but not distant enough. The skies signalled changing times with the smoke of burning settlements. The hermit brothers would have gathered together to discern the right path through all that precariousness. They could have insisted on staying and dying in their solitary dwellings on the mountain. Then they might have been remembered as martyrs to this day, and celebrated as exemplars of tenaciously staying rooted to the place they were called to be. Some may well have favoured that option as though their souls depended on it: fidelity forever anchored to location. There's no record of the men's conversation and the likely contest of views and visions. There is clear evidence of a conclusion. They may have arrived at their decision simply among themselves or in response to a directive from the local church authority. The Carmelites came down from their mountain.

They started a long march to Europe, and as they walked, they pondered who they were now that they had lost the geographical measure and solitary rhythm of their lives. What did it mean to be a Carmelite when Mount Carmel was lost to the horizon? How could a man be given over to solitary pondering in the bustle of Europe? How much compromise was acceptable? What were the non-negotiables of the call and the identity? What pragmatic deals would have to be made to find a place, and a necessary validation, beyond the simple austerity of life in the desert?

New Carmelite communities were formed across

Europe. Church politics had an impact on their form of life. They were re-branded as a mendicant order, like the Franciscans and Dominicans, so they could now be of some practical ecclesiastical use in the role of travelling preachers.

Further pragmatic readjustments followed. Rules were mitigated. Religious routines were changed. And, in the constant adjusting to their times – and the real issues of justification and survival in the church – they cast their minds back to ancient times and claimed the Old Testament prophet Elijah as their own. It was the right narrative. The claim to an ancient prophetic zeal guaranteed their survival. But all the while, the memory of the mountain, the solitude of the caves and the gravitational claim of pondering rolled through the generations of Carmelites. So, their identity included the deep wound that only exiles know: beneath the pragmatic layers of change and adaptation, there remained an ache for that long departed world of the mountain.

CHAPTER THIRTY-FOUR

Lunch was a boisterous Irish affair when I first visited the community in Sydney. I had been overwhelmed and fascinated by the old men and their vigorous banter. This changed when the novitiate commenced. Now a lone voice was heard reading a chapter of a book while the rest of the community lined up for lunch, took their seats at the long table and ate in relative silence.

The novices were given the task of finding an appropriate book. It had to be light, entertaining and, at best, humorous. Lunch wasn't a time for any heavy-handed spirituality. As the reading went on, amidst the clutter of cutlery and murmured requests to pass the salt, there was an occasional guffaw, smirk or raised eyebrow at some choice line. But there were mixed feelings, in the community, about the reading. Some of the old men had far from happy memories of the stricter monastic days of their early religious life. Some experienced even the smallest incursion of anything resembling the old ways as a cause of aggravation.

Julian had chosen a book consisting of a series of essays written by famous English catholic authors. It was an unsurprising choice. Julian was English by birth and an avid reader of a number of the contributing writers. He was emphatically working through an essay by Evelyn Waugh when the author launched into a critical summation of the Irish character. It culminated in a reference to the questionable intellect of the Irish peasantry.

"That'll be enough reading for today Julian!" boomed Jimmy, in his official capacity as prior of the community. "And I think we will have a different book tomorrow."

This was met with a murmur of agreement from the other Irish at the table.

"Irish peasantry, is it!" Terry said with whimsical aggravation. "Did you hear that, Kieran?"

The old brother, at the end of the table, mumbled something and then chuckled. The voice of English judgement was not welcome in the dark confines of the friars' dining room. Julian put the book down and collected his lunch with a Cromwellian glimmer in his eyes. He had given one to the old Irishmen and notched up a point for his motherland. Best of all, he couldn't be faulted for it. He had just been obediently reading a book.

Conversation erupted once the reading ceased. There was a jostle of voices: the piping sound of Chris making some emphatic point; the mumbled aside of old Kieran at the end of the table; the Kiwi singsong of Errol who had just come in from tending his growing flock of goats; a Latin maxim from Michael reminding all that whatever is received is received according to the mode of the receiver; a contrarian intercession from Terry as he scratched his prophetic beard; an anecdote from JV concerning the early days of the Varroville community, when the friars were bog deep trying to run an unsuccessful piggery.

There was another younger priest in the community, a contemporary of Chris, who took a giggling delight in hearing Jimmy speak on just about any subject.

"Oh, Father James, Father, tell us about the time you were reported to Rome. Oh, go on Father. Go on tell us."

Jimmy required little coaxing to launch into a tale. In this case, the story involved some reactionary conservative who had written to Rome to report the grand orator for something he had once said. It wasn't a particularly unusual story. Hardline conservatives had taken to patrolling parishes on the lookout for anything they deemed to be on the wrong side of orthodoxy. This often resulted in an identification of nothing more than the ignorance of the letter-writing guardians of the one true, holy, catholic and apostolic church. These stories entertained some, but they left me dispirited. I hated church politics and dreaded the day that I would have to negotiate my way through its rocky terrain.

Dirty plates, cutlery, glasses and leftovers were piled through the hatch to the kitchen after lunch. The younger friars, including the novices, took turns feeding things through the sink-top dishwasher, and then drying and putting it all away. The remaining food went into the walk-in fridge. Once the job was finished, we went back to the novitiate while a number of the older friars went to bed for their customary afternoon siesta.

CHAPTER THIRTY-FIVE

Ivan, Julian and I made our way back to the novitiate building. The hour after the community meal was designated as a time for recreation. We seized the opportunity to recreate some sense of the free-flowing exuberance we had known as postulants in Melbourne. Hansie took his recreation at a safe distance from our noise and general youthfulness.

"Put on the radio, bloody!" Ivan commanded as he raced off to his room. The building's timber frame shook as he propelled himself down the hall.

Ivan had started emphasising his ethnicity by regularly finishing his sentences with the word bloody. And so he might be heard asking with his signature mellifluous tone: "What's the time, bloody?" Or he might jolt us to action stations with the warning: "Paddy's coming, bloody!" And on rare occasions when we were able to head to populated areas, he could be heard strongly suggesting: "We're going to Smithfield, bloody. They have the best kebabs."

We put on the radio and the initial heartbeat rhythm of 'In the Air Tonight' filled the lounge. Ivan immediately ran back down the hall wearing nothing but his scapular and underpants.

"Phil!" he cried as though greeting a long-lost friend. He jumped on a chair and started playing his imaginary drum kit. His hands worked up and down in rhythm with Phil. His face was clenched with a pent-up intensity waiting for the great surge to come.

"Wait for it, bloody!" he advised. "Where's Linda? She has to be here!"

Julian then raced down the hall and brought Linda into the room. Ivan pointed an imaginary drumstick towards her in an act of sultry dedication. Linda stared back with her warm, sleepy eyes. Then the explosion came. Ivan's arms furiously moved around striking imaginary drum skins and cymbals. We were all yelling the words of the song; all feeling that dark mythic it that was coming in the air tonight. We shot occasional glances towards Linda, whose appearance never changed. The musical surge busted the stitched-up routine of our day. We sang with all the intensity we could muster and then sat back in our chairs and waited to catch our breath and the next wave of music.

"Hey, let's have a drink," Ivan said.

He wandered back to his room then returned with a sizeable bottle that was full of a clear liquid.

"What's that?" Julian asked.

"Rakija," Ivan said with a smile. "It's Dad's homebrew. It's good shit. Go get some mugs."

I went and collected three mugs from the kitchen, and then he poured.

"Nazdravlje!" Ivan toasted.

"Cheers," we replied.

The shot delivered a cascade of intense heat down my throat. It was potent like vodka and could strip paint off a wall.

"Another?" Ivan asked.

"Sure."

We took another shot and then Ivan returned the contraband bottle to a hiding place in his room. I could feel the heat lingering inside me and I felt mildly surrendered to a warm and happy place.

Linda didn't have a drink. She just sat in the lounge with her beckoning eyes and her sleep ruffled hair and the eternal guarantee that sleeping with her was a wonderfully warm experience. She might have been a discarded cardboard package for an electric blanket to the outside world, but she had assumed a greater status for us. Linda was the pin-up girl painted on the side of our celibate-bound novitiate, a mythical reminder of who and what we were leaving behind: a sultry goddess bound to be our undoing if we stopped for long enough to give her too much consideration.

CHAPTER THIRTY-SIX

Winter had given way to spring, and Chris was on to lead prayer and act as principal celebrant at the community mass for the week. He went about the business with an anglophile's brisk manner: the voice of a junior officer rousing the men to go off and die for king and country. This provoked a mumbling, tutting consternation among the old Irishmen, particularly when the young priest applied a variation to the standard way catholics made the sign of the cross.

"In the name of God: Father, Son and Holy Ghost," he declared, while his hand moved in an equally robust manner.

"Amen," the old men drily replied.

I could see their minds at work, under their furrowed brows, as they hunkered down for the morning's worship. It was such a tiresome business when young men felt compelled to make a point in the early hours of the morning. Surely it was enough to just get the business done without distracting fanfare or the assertion of a boisterous young ego.

We observed the scene as novices. There was the reality of the larger community: an often-muted grind of personalities played out in a religious arena. We were fascinated by the clashes, the bitchy asides, the evidence of a world that wasn't quite one mind and heart. It gave us something to gossip about at recreation and laugh about when the daily trials were heavy on our shoulders.

Chris was our Exhibit A as to what it meant to be a

young Carmelite priest. Discerning a sense of belonging was often a comparative process. How am I like this or that friar? How am I different? Does the difference matter? Is the likeness important? When I looked at Chris, I knew there wasn't an anglophile bone in my body. I wasn't inclined to the style of liturgy that he enthusiastically described as "bells and smells." He didn't have the peacefulness that I wanted and saw most clearly in Ryan. But there was an honesty in Chris's searching. It often sounded out when he led our morning classes. I took the things he said to heart. They stayed in me for years to come.

"When we look at the early Genesis narrative: Adam and Eve and the garden," Chris said one morning, "then we see that shame is the alienating force. It's shame that distorts perspective, that warps our natural and right understanding of God. It's shame that compels the person to run, to hide, to cover nakedness, to see the body as problematic. Shame compels the individual, or in this case the couple, to see truth – the divine presence that is truth – as a threatening thing. Shame says that truth is a threat to survival. Shame compels us to hide our true nature. Real grace is the dissolution of shame. Real grace joyously enables truth, true reality, true nature, to be not just faced but fully embraced."

Chris went into the city once a week. He usually left in the early afternoon and came back late at night. We knew he carried out AIDS ministry. It was 1990 and the epidemic was still hitting the gay community hard. He didn't speak directly about what he was doing or experiencing. We didn't ask. Chris's weekly absence was just a background event in our routine.

He left a candle burning, one night, in his room when he left to go to the city. I imagined it was for someone he knew. Maybe a light to help that person in the final hours of their life. Chris was into symbols in a major way.

Julian stormed into the room, once he knew Chris was gone, and blew it out. "That idiot could burn down the novitiate with his nonsense!" he declared.

There was a photo on Chris's desk. It showed an ecstatically happy young man in what seemed to be a nightclub with friends. There was something beautiful about the photo. It showed a fusion of joy and truth. It showed a happy Chris. He was free and alive in a way that he wasn't in the monastery. It made me think about his reflection on Genesis and the reality of shame and grace.

Maybe his words about the destructive nature of shame echoed words that other people had said to him. Maybe the presumption of his ministry had crumbled in the greater give and take of personal truths shared in the face of death. Maybe his ultimate experience of grace was the grace of other people who saw him truly and so helped him come home to himself after a long journey.

The monastery received a gift some time later. It was a statue of Mary. The thick limbs and general bulk of the figure was reminiscent of an early Magna Mater. It was Mary as I had never seen her before, full of the grace of a sumo wrestler, and not interested in budging an inch. Her eyes stared towards the retreat centre in a manner that was both vacuous and menacing. She was a gift from a too generous patron and was posited beside a cluster of bamboo on the front lawn where she waited to receive a suitable blessing.

There had been debate, in the main community, about how to proceed. Old JV had been nominated as the one to perform the blessing. He favoured something discrete. Chris was keen on a fuller celebration of the event involving a robust procession, hymn singing and all the liturgical accoutrements.

A young retreatant had an unfortunate accident involving his medication, sometime before the blessing, so an ambulance crept up the drive with lights flashing, just as the procession commenced across the front lawn. It was a vivid scene: an ugly statue demanding obeisance; a South West Sydney stab at Roman pageantry; Julian sending an incense-loaded thirible arching magnificently through the air; assorted friars processing in frilly ecclesiastical frocks; true believers from the parish and lay-Carmelite community shakily singing hymns while stepping over patches of mud; and all combined with the flourish of an unfolding medical emergency in the background. It would have delighted Fellini himself.

It was October. We had been in the novitiate for four months. Chris asked us to join him in the lounge room. He had something to tell us. It was the afternoon and an unusual time for any kind of announcement. That sort of thing happened in the morning class at the end room. We sat down on the couches and Chris got straight to the point as was his custom.

"I'm leaving the order effective immediately," he said.

There was a moment of stunned silence. It was inevitable that somebody was going to leave the novitiate but none of us had thought the assistant novice master would be the first to go.

"But why?" Julian asked.

"This place is never going to change," Chris replied. "Any attempt at renewal is just a hopeless cause and I can't see any likelihood of improvement in the foreseeable future. Really, the order is doing little more than shuffling deck chairs on the Titanic."

I sat there and wondered if the ship hit the iceberg before I had got on board or if it was a more recent catastrophe. It was almost impossible to know. And, taking the metaphor further, surely Chris had been the one who sold me the ticket to get on board in the first place. The marvellous life he had described in the letters I avidly read when I was still in Hobart apparently no longer existed. Maybe it never had. Deck chairs were being shuffled. The ship was going belly up. The band was playing on. The troubling waters were beckoning once again. Now he was jumping overboard.

I was stunned but I couldn't be angry with the man. There was that photo of him. All the frustrations we were hearing now were surely just the birth noise of his emerging truth and happiness, and I wanted that for him. There was courage in what he was doing. And yet there was a great implication in all this. It sat heavy in my mind. If the structured world of the church wasn't a sure and certain way to truth, then what was? If grace could lead a man to take lifelong vows, be ordained a priest and then leave, then what did that say about the church's claim to be the realisation of grace in the world?

I stood beside him, looking out the front door of the novitiate, after he had finished speaking to all of us. He told me that he didn't know what I should do, but he wished me well, and then he lumbered down the stairs with his bags and was gone. The world of the novitiate contracted as he walked away. Now there were just the four novices, the likelihood of an even more melancholic Paddy, and the emerging question of who would be next to leave.

CHAPTER THIRTY-SEVEN

It was Thursday and we were on the road with nothing behind us and everything ahead of us. Our heads were full of the mad rush and burn of an afternoon away from the novitiate. We'd thrown off the institution. Enough with medieval cross-dressing. The brown baggy encumbrance of our habits flew through the air as we changed in our rooms and declared ourselves new men in T-shirts and jeans and worn, old sneakers.

We had raided the main community lounge like a band of desperate villains, pilfering stubbies of beer and no-name potato chips, with someone on the lookout for old men on the horizon. Booze, cheap junk food, and a barely roadworthy vehicle. What else was needed to find our way to joy?

Midday prayer was done. Lunch was done. We said goodbye to Varroville, Campbelltown and the last vestige of suburban Sydney. We looked ahead as the great scrubby plain, down Appin Road, opened a world of sandy freedom to our eyes.

"The road is life, bloody!" Ivan yelled out the window with a wild passion that Kerouac would have been proud to call his own.

"Slow down, man!" Hansie yelled.

"We're fine, bloody. Keep your shirt on, old man!" Ivan replied.

We were bound for the magical winding descent down Bulli Pass to our collective go-to place on the coast. Austinmer: the name barely gave justice to the reality. I had been restless for days thinking about the beckoning blue expanse of the Pacific Ocean, the curl and suck of waves, the enveloping warmth of sand between my toes, and the reassuring evidence that an ordinary world still existed.

I knew, when I was on the coast, everything problematic in me would melt away: the stress, the self-consciousness, the panic attacks, the lurching sense of uncertainty in the wake of Chris's departure, the fatherland, the secret ballots, the dread of Paddy's grimace. I would be elementally unbound and free, fluid as the ocean, warm as the sun.

I had walked along the coastal road on previous Thursdays. It was good to set out and walk somewhere that was more than the cluster of hilly paddocks around the monastery. I had wandered through Coledale, Wombarra, Clifton and Coalcliff, and imagined living in one of those towns. I saw myself in some windswept raggedy house on a promontory. The ocean would be my companion day and night. I'd lay in bed listening to the waves. I'd rise at dawn and watch the sun push up from the ocean as I sipped my morning coffee. A coastal life would soothe and inspire me. I would write a book. The thought of that mythic other life lingered. Then all those impossible possibilities flew away with the sea breeze.

Ivan parked the car and we spilled out. Julian brought a rug which he threw down on the sand, and we deposited the beer and chips in the middle. First, we would eat and drink and then we would wander.

"Anyone want to see if there's a way up to a lookout?" Julian asked, as he gestured towards the escarpment that ran along the back of the town.

Ivan shook his head. Hansie also wasn't interested. He always went his own way. "Sure," I said. We walked through the backstreets of Austinmer and found a path into the escarpment forest. There was an overarching canopy of trees, a tangle of vines and the punctuation of bell-like purple flowers. It felt like an abundant and tropical Eden.

We walked along muddy tracks to see if we could reach some height that might offer a view of the coastline. At some point, our hands touched and then lingered. We glanced at each other. He smiled and so did I. It was safe. It was OK. There was delight in the connection, the light pressure of hands, the intermingling of fingers. The last time I had held hands with anyone was when I was a child. The only intimacy I had known was the hug and kiss of relatives. This wasn't the same. There was a vulnerable trust about it – a discovery of some tentative fragile thing that needed to be kept safe and hidden.

What did it mean? I looked in the mirror in my room, next morning. There I was: a twenty-three-year-old man who could hold another man's hand with more than a small degree of genuine tenderness. Was this my truth? Was I gay? I had the kind of soft manner that meant I had copped my share of homophobic barbs over the years. And yet, I found my pleasure in the thought of women. I always had. My imagining and dreaming had always been about the soft welcome of a woman's body. At least that was so before I entered the monastery.

Since I entered religious life, I smothered any thoughts about sex in their first movement, like a firefighter smothering the onset of some catastrophic fire. I hadn't masturbated since my tell-all confession before I left Hobart, and that was nearly a year ago. The requirements of my spiritual destiny had subjugated my body to a status of irrelevance. Sexuality was a muted thing.

I searched my face in the mirror. Who was I? What did this mean? There was no torturous shame in me. I knew that much. The turn of events was perplexing. It threw up questions. We held hands. There was a feeling of tenderness. Now we exchanged smiles and glances that conveyed a hidden delight in that sense of connection. Maybe there was delight in the experience that we shared some private world. And yet I wasn't stirred up with any clear physical desire. My heart didn't race, and I didn't get hard when I saw him. Whatever this was, it didn't undo me with desire or leave me restless with wanting in the early morning hours. So, what was this thing between us? It was perplexing, yet I felt peaceful about it. Peacefully perplexed.

CHAPTER THIRTY-EIGHT

Spring was simple everywhere but the novitiate. Change was happening in a complicated way inside that timber-frame crucible. The repercussions of Chris's departure were immediate. Paddy was around more often. He left for the parish directly after breakfast, but then returned to lead the novitiate class.

He started the classes with a long reading from his favourite spiritual writer Henri Nouwen. Paddy's favourite passages invariably referred to wounded healers, the problem of fear blocking intimacy, and the idea that solitude is being alone with the alone. Paddy softly cooed alone and lonely as though sounding out a sad yet sacred space in which he was most familiar.

Many of these ideas resonated in the fractured regions I felt inside myself. Maybe my real destiny was in becoming a wounded healer. I wanted to respond to the passages Paddy read, but I couldn't bear to speak up and see the old man's face disintegrate into that grimace of despair. It was one thing to read a passage on brokenness. It was another thing to hear the shaken sound of my voice revealing brokenness. My heart hammered furiously at just the thought of saying something when Paddy led the class. Fear indeed blocks the way to intimacy.

Paddy's greater presence wasn't the only change in the place. Julian was changing in a way I struggled to comprehend. One minute he was my friend with all those traces of trust and intimate connection that we had experienced walking at the coast. The next minute he was a jail guard desperate to control me. It was as though he saw our friendship as an undetonated bomb, and I was the one who would blow him up unless I kept my mouth shut, kept the friendship under wraps, stopped being silly or naive, and stopped trusting other members of the order who could never be trusted.

Ivan was changing too. He was preoccupied with events far beyond the little world of the novitiate. His mind was in Croatia where the claim of national sovereignty had collided with internal pockets of Serbian resistance. Ivan followed every piece of news in the daily papers. He restlessly watched news footage of Slobodan Milosevic talking up a greater Serbia, while accusing Croatians of fascism. He passionately tried to explain the complicated history of his country to his clueless brother novices. He made phone calls home that culminated in impassioned declarations of one kind or another in Croatian.

The horror of ethnic cleansing and massacre were just around the corner, and Ivan was starting to wonder why he was in a monastery when the world he really cared about was about to explode.

Ivan went looking for a suitable friend. He first met Friedrich Nietzsche at university. He was an old nineteenth-century German with a prominent moustache and a bad case of syphilis. Friedrich was bound for lunacy, but not before expounding his philosophy and the striking statement that God is dead. Ivan brought his old friend into the novitiate one afternoon and everything was suddenly questionable.

What was Christian virtue really about? Was it genuinely embracing and growing with life or was it the morality of a slave? How much are these religious structures and constrictions, the vows, the habit, the submission to some arbitrary power structure, all just about avoiding life? How much of all of this is just bullshit, fear, inhibition, a lack of daring to embrace the will to power? What are we really doing here when we could be anywhere, doing anything, being more than this?

The absurd dimensions of religious life no longer amused Ivan. He no longer channelled Phil Collins. He saw the cardboard Linda as a flimsy substitute for reality.

"I don't have time for this bullshit," he said. "What the flying fuck are we doing here in this place?"

Now he simply did what he wanted to do. He no longer let Paddy know about the money that his family sent. He used it when we went to Austinmer. He bought cigarettes for himself. He shouted us more than one beer at a coastal bikie pub. It was a final nostalgic taste of those old times when we were carefree postulants in Melbourne and the adventure of monastic life was still ahead of us. We drank our beer, ate our chips and talked about the experiences we had been through. His departure felt close, so every memory was vivid and available to be savoured. We had truly been brothers together.

Ivan casually left Nietzsche's *The Anti-Christ* on the coffee table in the novitiate lounge a few days later. Paddy came up the wooden steps after lunch, and through the sliding door.

"What's this?" he asked.

The old man was pale as a ghost when he saw it sitting there.

"I think Ivan's reading it," said Julian.

Paddy wandered off, knocked on Ivan's door, chatted for a while, and then the expected outcome happened. We all gathered in the kitchen.

"Paddy, would you like to try some of my rakija?" Ivan graciously asked.

"What's that?"

"It's a Croatian drink."

"Like poitin?"

"Probably so."

"And you have some here?"

"Yes, a bottle from my father."

"Well, I think we should have a drink then," Paddy replied, with a smile. Ivan came back with the generous bottle and poured a drink for everyone.

"Slainte," toasted Paddy.

"Slainte," we replied.

I kept busy when Ivan left. It was my best attempt at keeping the sadness at bay. I couldn't fake detachment. My humanity leaked like a sieve particularly after having more than one shot of the rakija. I cried when I said goodbye to him.

Hansie was incredulous.

"Surely you could see he was meant to leave? I mean, I don't know what the fuss is about man."

Paddy had taught a morning class on Saint Teresa's idea that spiritual beginners are like gardeners faced with a plot of barren soil and abominable weeds. God seeds virtue, and beginners need to make an effort to make the garden grow. The image had been playing through my mind every morning when I looked out my window. There was a tangled mess in front of the novitiate, where previous novices had grown vegetables. It was a mixed patch of dirt clods, rusted wire and rotting pieces of timber. It was riddled with ants and spiders. It was as barren and abominable as Teresa's image.

I wanted to drive away everything inside me. I set to work, dragging out coils of rusted chicken wire, stacking brittle timber stakes, collecting tetanus-primed old nails. I demolished mounds of hardened clay and threw ant colonies into chaos. The ants bit at my calves, but I didn't stop. It was hot and I was thirsty, but I just kept on. I hammered and clawed and racked and pulled until my T-shirt was saturated with sweat, until my heart beat too fast, until the angelus rang and I had to scramble off the mound to wash away the dirt and attend the midday prayers.

There was no joy in it. There was no satisfaction. Paddy expressed concern that I might be going at it too hard. I barely registered his tone of care. I told him I was fine. I thought this effort, at least, might prove I had some worth. He voiced a hope my efforts were a prelude to planting potatoes. I had no interest in planting anything. I didn't have that kind of hope. I just needed to keep busy.

Anger was never far away. I hated feeling the world shrink around me. I saw evidence of it every day in the empty rooms where Chris and Ivan had lived. Julian had gone in plundering the remains in the departed men's rooms. He had the scavenging inclination of a survivor and said we were in it for the long haul together. Just him and me. That's how it was now. I swallowed my doubts and agreed, but the future seemed starker now. The only thing left was to strike at the ugly earth, level it, and give its brittle fragments order. I worked for weeks until the job was done, and all the while, Friedrich Nietzsche sat on a tree stump laughing.

CHAPTER THIRTY-NINE

It was post-lunch recreation, but the days of loud music and dancing, under the watchful eyes of Linda, were now well and truly over. Julian was disgruntled. Again. We were walking along the narrow tracks in the back hills of the property. Again. He was debriefing about the inadequacies of the community. Again.

"They're not even bothering with a proper benediction at Sunday evening prayer anymore. The old men can't even be arsed putting on a cope to give the blessing."

I discovered it didn't help to joke about not coping with the absence of a cope.

"It might not seem like a big deal to you, Rob, but when small things are given up then, it's easier to give up more. It becomes a habit. Today it's the priests not wearing a cope. Tomorrow it's not bothering with benediction. And after that, it's not worrying about getting together for prayer at all, and hey, while we're at it, do we really need to have community mass every day? That's how the faith is lost Rob."

I found Julian's religious commitment exhausting. I was endeavouring to survive my mental world where an old man's grimace was the prelude to an inevitable rejection. Julian was fighting to survive his mental world where faith was imperilled by others' sloppy adherence to liturgical rubrics.

I sat in the chapel, that evening, as the world turned dark outside. There was no light but the flicker of the suspended sanctuary candle. I was often in the chapel beyond the two hours of private prayer specified in the monastic timetable. I sat in the corner and thought about my friendship with Julian. It now seemed weighted towards meeting his needs and keeping him placated, rather than sharing any kind of consoling and gentle connection. What did I care about whether a vestment was worn or not? I didn't, but he did, and he was my friend, so I had to try to care. I looked at the cross on the chapel's back wall. As it should be, I suppose. Loving as you love. Giving as you give. A crucifying submission to love's demands. There it was: the dark merry dance of the Christian mystery – words colliding and spinning with experiences, crucifixion, submission, limitation, loss, wanting. The image of the good shepherd holy card, in my child hands, suddenly came to mind. Holding. Hoping. Hoping that the holding might make some kind of difference.

My prayer had collapsed into one word since I entered the monastery. It was a raw word. It was utterly vulnerable and powerful. In fact, those two things were married together in it: vulnerable power, powerful vulnerability.

I prayed – *come* – and my mind drifted over the fragments and sharp, discordant edges of my life as a novice. The piecing together of what it meant to be a Carmelite. The piecing together of what it meant to be a true friend. The piecing together of what really mattered in the world of religion and religious practice. The piecing together of what kind of man I was.

Yet I was in the dark. I didn't know how my strange fragments were meant to be placed together

– *come*. I didn't know who I was. I didn't know how I was seen or judged by the community. I was silent. They were silent. They had their conversations about me behind closed doors – *come*. I didn't know when my likely rejection would happen. I suspected it might be soon. Ivan was gone. Surely, I was next in the firing line.

Was I praying for the end to come? I didn't know. The panic attacks had ground me down. My effort to be there as a friend for Julian was grinding me down. The feeling of inescapable judgement was grinding me down. I was praying for something that I didn't know, that I couldn't imagine or see, yet I had no choice but to do it. There was just this hunger stretched into a word. I was praying – *come* - but to what or who? You? Whatever I was praying for, it felt like life and death and weakness and strength were bound together in it. It came from ground-down me. It came from near-drowned me. It came from resilient me. It came from determined me. It came from every disparate fragment that was me. The whole shattered, splintered span. My life. My death. Everyone else's: gathering into me and me into you.

I looked across the chapel at the place where I had prayed for you to tell me if I was meant to join the order. I remembered my mind and how it was awash with Jimmy's preaching: creation from the watery chaos, the dislocating struggle in the water for a blessing, the grip of stories, the power of narrative.

Now I sat and listened. Ancient Irenaeus of Lyon

came out of the dark and whispered in my mind. He was my old friend. I knew him before I joined the order.

The word from the early church saint and theologian drifted through my thoughts. Recapitulation: it's such a clumsy, awkward word. But in all the words I had come to hear and know, this one was mine. It settled in my mind as I sat in the chapel. I kept it. I held it. I prayed my one word – *come*. It struck against this other clumsy word and sent up sparks. I knew this word of hope would last me years. It would last me to my final breath. It would stretch right through my life and capture everything: all the pieces, dispelled and seemingly apart, the dark space of contradictions, all the vast, expanding universe, everything named and unnamed, dark and far from home, moving towards a single point of gravity – a morning star, a kindly light, home.

I wanted home, but I didn't know where it was anymore, except in this strange moment of reaching through the dark. I looked across the chapel. Jesus was on his cross. The sacrament was in the tabernacle. A cow was bellowing for its calf in some distant paddock. A hoon was flooring a stolen car up the dark road down below. I told myself this was what it meant to be at the heart of the church, caught at the beginning and end of a pulse, listening to the murmuring of saints and sparking hope from what I gleaned. I told myself tonight, at least, I am a Carmelite.

CHAPTER FORTY

There was a quivering edge in Paddy's voice as he asked me and Julian to stay back at the end of the morning class. Hansie wandered down the hall to his room. There was an awkward moment of silence. Paddy sighed. He frowned. He sighed again. His eyes looked up: a fleeting moment of eye contact turned into a middle-distance stare. "There's some concern in the community that the two of you are forming a particular friendship," he said, "There's concern that there might be a dependence."

He left the final word hanging in the air. It was loaded with significance and none of it was good. In spiritual terms it suggested a reliance on something other than God which would prevent spiritual growth. In hackneyed psychological terms, it suggested a weakness – the need for a crutch to get along, an insufficiency of strength and self-reliance.

"The two of you are together an awful lot," Paddy concluded, with a tremulous emphasis that suggested this was the evidentiary foundation of the judgement.

"But we're novices," Julian protested. "There's just the two of us and Hansie."

"Nevertheless," a now-irritated Paddy disrupted, "concern has been raised, and it has been decided it would be good for you to spend less time together. Robert, I've arranged for you to help Errol reorganise the bookshop storage room in the afternoons. You can start today."

I looked across the table at Paddy. All I could see and hear was the fatherland passing its judgements and issuing its decrees from the other side of a terrible divide. The merest suggestion that there might be further discussion of the matter was crushed under heal. Rightness and belonging were predicated on the expectation of a quiet compliance. Order was everything.

I spent my afternoon salvaging and stacking dusty, water-spoilt books and pamphlets in a closet-like space. I dare say no irony was intended. I sat on the concrete floor, in that too familiar state of isolation, angered at the thought that this was what you wanted. After all, you supposedly spoke through the voice of my novice master. His directions were your directions: your grace married to the structure and performance of roles; your formative hand in the judgements and decrees of the old men.

Yet I had hoped for something else when I came into the monastery: the better world, beyond the border of the fatherland, where stories are shared and paths are plotted through the journey of real conversations. The better world where fears are conquered by growing trust and where divides are bridged by a shared passion to know the other. The better world where I could clearly see and speak my truth, whatever truth you had written in my soul, and feel myself deep-rooted and right in the world, and therefore there for others as I found others had been there for me. The better world where I would have run to catch a bus to sit with a long-ago friend and found the way to meet him in his loneliness. The better world where good shepherds turned up when needed and did something a little more useful than die. The better world. The better me. The better you. My friendship with Julian was my first tentative step in seeking that world. The friendship wasn't perfect. It was increasingly challenging and sometimes bruising, but it was where I had begun to connect with someone. I had hoped and trusted in that world – and in you and your kingdom promises. I had hoped and trusted, and it landed me on my arse, on cold concrete, in the isolation of a musty little room.

CHAPTER FORTY-ONE

Another day and another after-class intervention by Paddy. I braced myself for the worst. It didn't matter that I'd spent every weekday afternoon in the confines of a musty closet sorting water-damaged books that were good for nothing but recycling. Nothing really mattered. Fault could be found anywhere, and it would be. I was sure of that. My clock was counting down. My forced departure was surely imminent. I looked at Paddy's careworn face and waited for the fatherland to speak.

"So," Paddy began, with an exaggerated smile which was possibly more unnerving than the grimace. "I have some news. I've decided you should both do some pastoral work while you're here. Just a little thing really. I've organised for you both to teach catechism at one of the government schools down the road."

"What grade?" Julian asked.

"Older children. I think grade six."

"When?"

"Soon. You need to go and speak to sister down at the parish. She's the one to organise these things. And what do you have to say, Rab?"

I faked enthusiasm and said it could be a good experience. I was glad the old man couldn't see into my mind which was now in a catastrophising frenzy. It was one thing to plummet into the death spiral of panic attacks in front of the friars. I had reached a point, after more than six months, where I was able to maintain a relatively smooth veneer over my general state of clammy desperation. I wasn't sure the veneer would last in the radically different situation of a school classroom, and I knew that falling apart in front of a roomful of twelve-year-olds would be the ultimate humiliation. I looked across at the old man and wondered if that was his devilish plan: a shameful knockout blow that would leave me with no choice but to leave.

Meanwhile Julian was invigorated as he imagined teaching a pack of unchurched school kids, before they were lost forever to secularism and the onset of adolescent hormones.

"It's an opportunity for these kids to get solid doctrine about their catholic faith. Just some basics at least: the sacraments, the real presence, why Jesus died on the cross, sin and forgiveness."

"I wonder what they might know already," I tentatively offered.

"They won't have a clue. Come on, Rob. Half of these kids probably haven't even set foot in a church since they were baptised."

"But still ..."

"This is the one chance these kids will have to learn about their faith. Even if it makes a difference to one of those kids, it's worth it," he concluded.

"I think we should start with finding out what their experience of God and their spiritual life is," I said, with a surprising degree of assertion. Where did that come from?

"God, Rob," Julian retorted, "all those kids have ever been given is touchy feely reflections. You can be sure nobody's ever taught them the basics. That's the difference we can make."

"I think ..."

"Alright, the first class we can try your way, but then we'll get on with teaching them some solid catholic teaching."

I let the condescension pass. It was my first experience of how different our pastoral instincts were.

Julian didn't have a driver's licence, so I drove us to the school a few weeks later. It was the first time I had set foot in a primary school since my own childhood. I felt a shudder pass through me. I was surprised such an ancient feeling could so promptly reemerge: the child's leaden dread now in the belly of a man; the thread of nocturnal panic weaving through my current moment; the child voice inside me pleading to walk out the door and never come back. There was no place more dreadful than a school.

I stood in the entrance hall and looked around. I heard the sound of children's boisterous joy. They were safe and happy enough to greet their school day with exuberance. The hall was bathed in generous sunlight. There were no rickety stairs and no foreboding shadows. I listened for the faintest hint of malevolence: some sharp barb from a teacher, a callous put-down, a regimental decree, a threat of violence to come. I couldn't hear anything like that. It was extraordinary. There was ease between the children and their teachers. There was an air of confidence and trust. This was not the place I once was. If anything, this was some small instance of the better world: a government school with little to no religion. I realised I would be OK today. I realised I was safe enough to breath.

We stood at the front of the class. The children's eyes shone with an inquisitive wonder as they looked up at these two young men dressed like characters out of Robin Hood. We introduced ourselves.

"Hi, I'm Brother Julian."

"And I'm Brother Robert."

A hand shot up.

"Why are you in costumes?"

"Well, it's a special costume called a habit. Has anybody heard of a habit?" Julian asked.

"My dad smokes. That's a bad habit."

"Yes. That's a different kind of habit," replied Julian, with a stage chuckle. "But, for us, a habit is the thing we wear, and it says we belong to a religious order. Does anyone know what a religious order is?"

The class stared blankly at us.

"Sometimes God calls people to live together and spend their lives doing special jobs for the church. Our order's called the Carmelites, and our main job is to pray. Does anyone know any prayers?"

"The Our Father," said a girl near the front.

"That's right," said Julian, "maybe we can start our class praying it together."

He made a great sweeping sign of the cross, pressed the palms of his hands together, and then launched into the slowest rendition of the Lord's Prayer I had ever heard. The few kids who knew the prayer were left tripping over themselves, as they realised they had surged too far ahead of the strange, tall, serious man in the brown dress. The majority of kids mumbled their best approximation of a prayerful noise. Never had an amen been so welcome.

Julian then gave me a nod. I stepped forward with a pile of A4 pages in my hands. I passed out the piles to the front row and told the kids to pass them back. I was busy and the kids were cooperating, and I didn't register that my nerves and self-consciousness had fallen away.

"Now," I said, "do you all have coloured pencils?" There was a room full of nodding heads.

"I want you to draw how God is part of your life. Do you think you can have a go at that?"

They got to work with their coloured pencils. Heads down, hands vigorously drawing and shading. As I walked along the row of desks, I saw a great diversity of pictures emerging. Some showed a classic bearded Jesus holding hands with a child or pictures of doves hovering over the heads of happy families. Some took the Mickey out of the whole exercise with random scribbles accompanied by sniggering. Other works were surreal depictions of scenes involving heaven, dead grandparents, angels and rays of golden light. Overall it represented the broad world of twelve-year-old kids' beliefs, attitudes and perceptions. I gathered up the pictures at the end of class and felt like I had established a foundation for building understanding. The pictures were a strange, pastel-coloured starting point.

Julian was in charge the following week. He walked to the front of the class, held up his small crucifix, and declared to the miniature pagan horde: "This is how much God loves you!"

It was a scene reminiscent of a holy card. The only thing that was missing was a beam of light to illuminate his tall frame in the suburban pagan darkness. One child replied "Yuk!" in response to dead Jesus. I smiled. It was the most concise critique of Christianity I had ever heard.

I was standing to the side with my own doubts. I was on board with the idea of sacrifice related to parents going without so their children can have more, or athletes making sacrifices so they can dedicate their time and energy to their discipline. Sacrifice that's a costly form of generosity or a measure of dedication was fine. But I had always had trouble with sacrificial thinking that had even a vague hint of throwing a baby goat into a volcano, in the hope it might be satisfied with the offering and therefore decide not to rain down a hellish storm of molten lava.

"Did God want Jesus to die like that?" asked an eager child in the corner.

"Well, yes. It was something that needed to happen," Julian replied.

"Why?"

"Because, well, we all sometimes do the wrong thing don't we?"

There were some less than enthusiastic nods.

"Jesus wasn't like that. He always did the right thing. Now, the real test of doing the right thing is when it's hard, isn't it? Well, Jesus did the right thing even when he faced the hardest thing: dying a really painful death."

The room was silent.

"He gave himself for us. He did the right thing to make up for all the times we have done the wrong thing."

Silence.

"He died for all of us, for everyone in this class, and everyone in the world, and everyone going all the way back through time."

Silence and frowning.

The class went on with Julian working his themes. Jesus' sacrifice then led into discussion of mass and the eucharist. He presented his points and then reframed them. A few eager kids answered questions, but most sat there nonplussed. Relief finally came with the sound of the bell.

"Well, I think that went well," Julian said, as we drove back to the monastery. I really didn't know what to say.

"Don't you think?" he asked.

"Well, I think the theology of the cross is tough for all of us."

"It's the heart of what we believe."

"Hmm."

"Well, how could I have done it differently?"

"I don't know."

"What then? Do you think we should just ask them to draw lovely pictures and avoid trying to teach what the faith's really about? It's such a cop out, Rob. You can do better than that."

I had no reply. Maybe he was right. Maybe I was prone to avoid teaching difficult ideas. Maybe I was a shirker when it came to communicating the hard Christian doctrine that confronts like the scandal of the cross. He was definite and direct. His sense of truth was bound in church teaching: a thick catechetical instruction manual of Christian belief that needed to be taught to people in their ignorance. Once they mastered the manual, they would know their way around the grand machine of orthodoxy constructed over the course of two thousand years by reliable and preferably holy mechanics inspired by the Holy Spirit. And God was presumably somewhere in the design of it all, the grand accrual of an intellectual legacy, the interconnecting perfection of one part logically following another. It inspired the wonder of an engineer.

If I was certain of one thing, it was that I was not an engineer. My sense of truth looked towards something that was inside people, waiting to be uncovered and shared. It reached back to my five-year-old self, sitting in a classroom, listening to the parish priest tell parable stories. My appetite was for stories, exploding starting points for thinking that spread in all directions, like flowers breaking open to the sun. I trusted something that was vague, shared thoughts that stretched the mind with more questions than answers, the triggering moments that awakened something deep within the heart, a love that can't quite explain itself but that nevertheless is.

CHAPTER FORTY-TWO

Julian came into my room. His bony, flexing cheeks and flared nostrils flagged there was a problem. That wasn't unusual. Every day delivered a problem even though a major overhaul had occurred in the tumultuous life of our novitiate. Paddy was no longer the novice master. A relatively younger priest, Henry, had come over from the community in Western Australia to take over the role. Henry was a gentle man. He brought a soothing spirit to the place and seemed focused on establishing a genuine connection with his charges.

I had started breathing a little easier. I no longer had to contend directly with Paddy's grimace. My chance of surviving novitiate seemed better with Henry in charge.

"Have you talked to Sam since he arrived?" Julian asked with an accusatory edge.

Sam had come up from the Melbourne student house. He was going to be the chief chef for the community's Christmas lunch. He embraced the role with a kind of complaining delight. I was glad to see him. He dragooned me into the role of wrapping wontons for the festivities. I was happy learning an exotic new skill and having the chance to engage in friendly banter with someone I trusted.

"I haven't really talked to him much. Why?" I asked Julian.

"Just be careful. He's sniffing around trying to get the lowdown about what's going on in the novitiate. What's he said to you?"

"Well, he asked me how I was going."

"And?"

"I said there's been ups and downs." Then I said, "Sam's alright."

Julian's face twisted into a tenser knot. "You're too trusting Rob. You think people are like you. They're not. Sometimes you're so naive. You know what Finch says about old Sammy – he's as cunning as a shithouse rat."

I didn't respond. He saw I needed further convincing. "I was talking to him last night," Julian continued.

"Oh."

"If you knew what he'd said about you then you wouldn't be so trusting."

I flinched at the provocation. I knew I'd regret asking but I did anyway. "What did he say?"

"Sam told me he thinks you're weak-willed. That's what he really thinks of you. You're weak-willed and easily led. They were his exact words. And if he said that to me, then you can be sure he said the same or worse to others in the community."

Julian's revelation was a sharp barb. It twisted inside me. I liked and trusted Sam, but I didn't doubt Julian's account of that conversation. It sounded like the kind of privately shared assessment I had heard Sam pronounce about others, at various times, when I was a postulant.

I imagined him with Julian. They probably went out for a walk together. Sam undoubtedly asked him what was going on in the novitiate with a tone of grave concern. That's what Sam had done with me during a clumsy game of snooker the night before. He would have listened to Julian with that concentrated knot he gets between his eyebrows, intensely taking it all in.

Sam would have been quiet for a moment then said something like, "I'm not sure it's my place to say what I know." He often came out with the type of line that asserted his significance as a gatekeeper of insider knowledge. *Should I say this? Maybe it's best I didn't.* It was as though he needed to exhibit some wrestling with his conscience to emphasise his words were not pronounced lightly. He'd say the thing he had always intended to say, with a frown and a tone of serious concern and with an accompanying humble footnote that this was just his view and he could, of course, be wrong.

I had felt an insider's pleasure, as a postulant, when Sam shared his views with me. It was surely an act of trust, so maybe I could trust him in turn and tell him those things I really thought and felt. Now I knew what he really thought of me. Maybe he was busy assessing me in those moments of apparent connection. Maybe he had been gauging the strength of my will in everything I had said to him. Maybe that was the real agenda behind all those friendly chats. My moments of trust had been nothing more than a demonstration of my weak will and my tendency to be easily led. He had gathered the evidence and now he had passed his judgement.

At least I finally had some definite words for the judgement that I felt every day in the novitiate. How often had the friars said something similar about me behind their closed doors? And how could I refute it anyway? Surely it hurt because it was true. How often did I speak up about what I really thought and felt? How often did I swallow my opinions for the sake of avoiding conflict? How often did I let someone else take the lead, someone like Julian, so I could avoid the drama of negotiating with an overwhelming world? How often did I simply presume that other people knew better than me?

I knew I was weak. I knew it long before I joined the order and, in the novitiate, the knowledge was amplified every day. How could it not be when authority and judgement were embedded in the structure of the life? I had tried to hide my weakness, but I obviously failed. I had trusted and that had yet again proven me a fool. Weak-willed and easily lead. The words burnt like acid, and the fact Sam shared this view with Julian made it all the worse. I wondered what Julian had said in that conversation. Had he agreed with Sam's judgement or had he tried to refute it? That was another conversation behind closed doors. I laid in bed that night and wondered if I could trust anyone in that world. Including myself. Including you.

CHAPTER FORTY-THREE

The familiar curves of Mum's schoolgirl handwriting and the loving intent of her letters made my universe slightly better. I was often the first to check the letterbox when I heard the mailman barrelling up the road. Most days I trudged up the driveway with disappointment and a pile of letters for other people. A letter was a slice of normality, a touchstone to the world that I had left, and a reassurance that I hadn't completely fallen off the family radar.

One of Mum's letters arrived just before I was due to go and ring the midday angelus. I had enough time to stop in my room and feel that briefest connection with home. I sat down, opened the envelope, and unfolded the small pages. "Darl, I'm so sorry, but I have some bad news to tell you," it began. My eyes raced across the page until it was too much to bear.

I was still at university when my middle brother Steve made his first suicide attempt. I had kept a certain distance from it all: the late night phone call, my parents' panic, the rush to hospital emergency, his later arrival back home with his wrists bandaged up, his vacuous eyes, his silent still body lying on the bed in the front room. He was just an empty shell surrounded by desperate family members not knowing what to do.

He was fourteen years older than me. We weren't close. I had grown up aware of the scowl that often crossed his face when he saw me. I presumed it was a look of judgement: I was the over-sensitive baby brother, spoilt and mollycoddled, a creature that provoked him to shake his head with cynical bemusement. I never understood why the judgement was there or what it meant. My childhood traversed an often-obscure landscape laid down by the older members of my family.

My brother was drawn to the visceral side of life: the business of shit and blood and mortality, the kind of things that made people squirm, the kind of squirming that caused him to smile. He walked the Midlands paddocks, near his family home, setting rabbit traps on certain evenings. He'd talk about the way the bunnies screamed when the traps snapped on their legs and sealed their fate. He relished the application of a blade, the slide of a knife parting skin from meat, the vigorous thrust to gut and clean, the fall of mangled innards, the disjointing dig and push to section the prey and make it ready to cook and eat.

He had more than a small measure of his grandfather, the butcher, in him. He could have gone down that road. It might have worked for him. Or he could have been a doctor or a nurse. Anything involving a hands-on immersion in the bloody negotiation between life and death. But he didn't go down any of those paths. He was a public servant for a time. Then he tried to start a consultancy business that failed. He closed himself off with the failure and drank until his hope seeped away. He used his knife skills in a different way then and nearly ended everything.

So, he was bandaged and catatonic on a bed, and I was in my bedroom out the back.

Mum suddenly hollered with such concentrated

panic it jarred me to the bone, and I ran out. "He's gone," she said, "quick you need to follow him. We need to know where he is." I flew out the front door and could see him walking up the hill. Lazarus risen from the dead and walking with a sense of purpose. I followed from a distance feeling nothing but anger. It was the first time in years that I had felt anything so vividly and I knew it was at odds with what I should feel. Where was my compassion? Where was my care? Where was my brotherly love?

I mumbled fuck you with every step. I directed it at the back of his dull head as I followed him, at a distance, up one hill and then another, and then down towards the bluff and the river. I wondered what I'd do if he tried something stupid like jumping in front of a car or trying to drown himself. Did I have it in me to overpower him? Was there anything near enough, between us, for me to convince him not to die?

My rage was a wild thing, twisting and bucking under my skin, grinding at my soul like the gravel under my feet. If my brother, who had so much, could come to this, then surely I could too. And if the choice of a normal life, with a wife and kids and a family home, was that precarious, then where could hope be found? What was there to live for if everything that I thought added up to a good life could crumble so easily? And if I stopped and thought about my own life, the meaningless years studying engineering, my diminishing confidence and growing social isolation as a university student, the lack of any sense of my life having any meaningful direction, then surely I had more reason to end my life than he did. His reasons seemed piss-weak to me, and I felt the strangest of all things: resentment. I looked at him with the cold, hard judgement I had often imagined he had directed towards me. I watched him walk into a pub, and I felt a black temptation of despair breathe right through me as I went to the phone booth and rang home to give them a report.

It all came back to me as I sat in the novitiate holding Mum's letter. I pictured what it was like down there: my brother sunk back inside himself and everyone walking on eggshells desperate not to rock the boat. It caught me like a wave, and I was left sobbing and rocking in the chair, wanting to reach out and console my mother who was so far away, wanting to be with my family in their need, wanting to be with people who cared, wanting to shake my brother until he woke up, wanting to smash the grip of contagious despair that always lurked in the shadows.

Julian walked in.

"What's wrong?"

"Steve, my brother, tried to kill himself."

"Oh shit. Is there anything you need me to do?"

"No. I don't think I can handle facing the community at lunch."

"That's OK. I can let them know, if that's what you want."

"I guess. I have to ring the angelus."

"I can do it."

"No. That's alright."

I was still sobbing when I walked across to the

chapel bell. I wasn't going to let any bastard find fault with me for failing to do my rostered duty. Three rings of three and one ring of nine. I channelled pain and rage into each pull of the rope. Here's your fucking angelus, I muttered as the bell rang out across the valley. Here's your fucking angelus.

I withdrew back to my room like a wounded animal. I sat in the chair in my bedroom staring into space. I had it in me to disintegrate into nothing or harden into fury. Henry came to my door. He looked startled as he stood there, like a rabbit in the headlights. He barely dared to come into my room. He hovered between an outreaching duty of care and not wanting to intrude.

"I'm sorry you've had this news," he said. "Has this happened before?"

"Yes."

"It's an awful thing. Often when a person's like that, they usually end up succeeding."

I stared at him not knowing how to respond. This wasn't helping. But my heart went out to him because he was a good man, with care and concern written all over his face, and he was trying.

"Do you think it might be helpful to have some space to yourself? I can organise some money. Maybe you can go into the city. Just get away from here and find some space."

I nodded.

I went into the city by train, with no idea what to do or why I was there. I went up the steps from the underground, at Town Hall Station, and surrendered to the flow of people: a paper boat washed along a gutter. I just walked. I couldn't think. I looked around perplexed at this strange, jostling world, the endless shops, the darting crowds, everything foreign to my eyes. There was no-one there for me. Not a single person. The only people who understood were more than a thousand kilometres away. I grew tired of walking. I went into a cinema at the grimy end of George Street. I just wanted to sit somewhere. I stared at the screen, barely registering what was going on. It didn't matter. None of it mattered. Nothing made sense.

I went back to Town Hall and got on a train after the movie finished. I returned to the monastery, ate on my own, and told myself I was going to join the community for night prayer. I went to the chapel, took my place, braced myself and chanted the psalms along with the community. And, when the prayers ended, the friars formed a line and each one gave me some expression of their care: a word of sorrowful concern, a silent grip of the shoulder, a promise of prayers for my family, the quick glance of Paddy's eyes close to tears, a raw moment of genuine community that briefly dissolved the scales on my eyes and hinted at a bond that might be real.

I wrote a letter to my brother later. I told him I hated what he had tried to do. I told him to get off his arse and find some reason to live and get on with it. That's what I had to do after I followed him down to the pub on that desolate afternoon in Hobart, long before I entered the monastery. He opened his wrists. I bled my own measure of despair. It set me on a course to find some reason to live, and here I was in a monastery. And if the community's vote on my staying or leaving the order felt like a life-or-death proposition, it was probably because it was. I knew the dark inside myself. It lurked at the deepest point of all my anxieties and fears. It lingered in my memories and the judgement that I felt all around me. Its presence was fierce as gravity. I was desperate for something greater than that darkness, a solid foundation for my life, the better world, something conventionally described as salvation.

PART FOUR

CHAPTER FORTY-FOUR

It was the end of September 1991. I was with Julian in the front bar of the Imperial Hotel in Melbourne. Novitiate had ended in July. In the language of the monastery, we were simply professed. We had taken religious vows of poverty, chastity and obedience for the next twelve months. We would take those three vows every year until the time came, in early 1996, when we were due to take them for life. We were the last two survivors of the novitiate group. Hansie left the order soon after we returned to Melbourne.

Money was limited, so we drank our pints slowly, as we watched a small television that was fixed above the window. It was quiet along Spring Street. Downtown Melbourne was empty compared to its normal Saturday bustle. There would have been plenty of noise if it had been any other Grand Final Day, but the MCG was out of commission due to construction, and the game was being played in the outer suburb of Waverley.

Hawthorn had always been my team. Their surgical precision was pure joy to me, and they weren't disappointing that afternoon. Old man Tuck, in his signature long-sleeved guernsey, was busy moving the ball out of halfback. He'd been in the brown-and-gold forever, and this was his last game.

"Carn Tuckey!" I yelled. "Bring it home you good thing!"

It felt good to be lost in a moment of normal, pure joy. Johnny 'The Rat' Platten, all hair and speed, wove into space, and fired one pass after another to Pritchard. Boot to ball, muscle, jostle, ferocity, the momentum of a body flinging another aside, a timely swing, a perfect handball, a dash, a glorious mark – brute perfect choreography.

I was lost in it. My heart thundered with a passion not just to win, but to strike repeatedly, to master with every point registered on the board, to trample the enemy in the mud and send the bastards back to the west with tears in their eyes. It mattered so much I could hardly stay in my seat. All the assertive action of the game was alive inside my body. All the dampened ferocity of my soul relished the liberation of this moment.

"JD!" I yelled as Dunstall took another signature chest mark thirty metres out from goal, then slammed the ball through the big posts. "You good boys, you mighty Hawks, you fucking legends!"

Julian caught the fever and revelled in the passion of it.

"Come on Hawks!" he yelled, turning to me with a grin plastered over his face. In that moment, he was a youthful, exuberant boy and the perfect mate to sip a beer with while yelling victoriously at the small screen. The exacting religious figure who got worked up over the finer points of liturgy seemed far away, and the vulnerable one I once held hands with seemed even further away.

And, for my part, I had slipped off the skin of my fractured, overwhelmed monastic self, as surely as I had thrown off the habit after the morning liturgy. I was just a twenty-four-year-old, mildly intoxicated lad, vicariously charged with the power of my football team's victory. I was a southerner who was finally back in the welcome cool embrace of the south, just a stretch of water away from my island, revelling in an ordinary world and a simple, clear passion.

We were heading home on the train along the Belgrave-Lilydale line in the evening. There was a great surge of people, all decked out in the team colours, getting off the train at Glenferrie.

"Come on, let's get off!" said Julian.

He was on his feet before I said a word. We followed the crowd down to the hemmed in little ground beside the train line. It was the old suburban homeground and still the spiritual home of the Hawks. The streets were brimful with euphoric supporters, a great dionysian cacophony of pure joy, cars blasting their horns in victory, drunk men arm in arm, brown and gold flags circling above, chants filling the air. I filled my lungs with the cool evening air and threw out the song lines with all the rest.

We're a happy team at Hawthorn.
We're the mighty fighting Hawks.
We love our club and we play to win,
 riding the bumps with a grin.

As we shuffled along, we could see the earlier arrivals had built a bonfire in the middle of the ground. Everyone was cheering as the flames spread up into the Melbourne night. A fire engine turned up and had to crawl behind the shuffling crowd on the road down to the ground. The chant went up again, then the firies started sounding their horn in unison. It was one of the best nights I'd ever experienced, and there was no place in the world I'd rather have been.

CHAPTER FORTY-FIVE

It was the first morning back at class. I had a full course load. It was a mix of philosophy, theology, history and scripture. I was looking forward to getting my teeth into something intellectual after a novitiate year that was more about survival than furthering knowledge. It was time to put all that behind me, though that was easier said than done. The long months of scrutiny and judgement had worn me down.

It was still hard to believe that I had survived novitiate. My worst expectations had proven wrong. Someone told me I was voted through based on how I weathered the news of my brother's attempted suicide. It was depressing to think that a decision about my future was based on that experience but I suspected there was some truth in what I was told. Persevering through dark times was the bread and butter of an order that had the dark night of the soul at the heart of its tradition. I imagine my perseverance through that challenging time trumped whatever other views had been tossed around behind closed doors when I was discussed as a novice: that I was weak-willed and lacking independence or a barely closeted homosexual or a psychiatric basket-case.

I had taken my temporary vows in the retreat centre chapel. My parents were there and numerous people who were connected to the order. It was a jolly gathering. Light streamed through the side windows and Michael, the head of the order in Australia, presided at the ceremony with the same gentle

Donegal murmur that I had heard when I received the habit.

The first profession of vows went without a hitch. My panic attacks had largely receded, so I didn't collapse in a state of nervous anxiety. When I stood outside, once the ceremony was over, I burst into tears. I had no idea relief could pack such an enormous wallop. I felt like a channel swimmer stumbling onto the beach. I had traversed the peaks and troughs of the fatherland for twelve long months. I had nearly drowned in my own anxiety on countless occasions. I had weathered the storm of other people's departures. Yet here I was. I had made it to the other side. I wanted to sob until I was spent, but a pious old man, who had just shaken my hand and congratulated me, suggested I needed to steady on a bit. Clearly the fatherland had to have the final word on that chapter of my life.

I was sure the greater truth was waiting to be found in the world of books and ideas, in the deep considerations of scripture and existence, in all the undercurrents that made the church what it was. It was time to plunge into the world of a theology student, piece together an understanding, study and pray and find my identity and rightful place in the church. And if I did well in my studies then my worth would finally be proven to the order.

I imagined the friars' backroom conversations about me shifting from negative to enthusiastic judgements. *Well, isn't that Robert coming along now. I always knew he had it in him. The quiet ones so often do, you know. Maybe we should send him overseas for his doctorate. Oxford? Washington? What about Spain? It might be good for him to get some Spanish under his belt and experience Avila and Salamanca firsthand. Let him know the places that have shaped our spirituality. What's that you say? Some time in Ireland would certainly round him off. Yes indeed. Maybe he could go to Trinity. He has an inclination to literature, you know, and where else could be better than Dublin for the boy. Sure a few years there would round him off just right.*

I allowed myself a moment to bask in my brilliant future, along with the order's ultimate warm embrace, as I walked the couple of hundred metres up the driveway to class.

Julian was mumbling beside me as he braced himself to pass through the jaws of that greatest of all hells, liberal catholicism, and into its academic den of iniquity. He had made some initial noises about wearing the habit to class. I had managed to put him off. The Carmelite students had never worn their habits regularly to class, and I wasn't interested in setting some new trend. But Julian had that brittle, determined look about him, and I knew the habit was a topic that we would be revisiting sometime soon.

Students shot past us, in their cars, eager for a favourable park. The college and the conjoined Franciscan residence was ahead. It was a long structure that erupted, at the car park end, in a multistorey high chapel of coloured glass and suburban orange bricks. There was a high belltower, overshadowing the chapel, crowned with one arch atop two supporting arches, but there were no bells in the tower and the cavernous space of the chapel was most often empty. The building became quite ominous at night: a desolate shell that was created to be full of life.

The entry to the college was through an unassuming back door behind the chapel. I walked through the building and into the morning light that spilled through the interior cloister. The consoling green of the central garden caught my eye. The place hadn't changed since my days as a postulant. Students were milling about, checking where their classes were, catching up on holiday experiences and speculating about the quality of lecturers. There were many people I didn't recognise and others whose names I had forgotten. I faked familiarity with a nod here and hallo there. Then I saw Mia in the crowd. She was a friend from my days as a postulant. I felt an unexpected sense of relief. She looked up at me and smiled. I momentarily forgot to breathe.

"You're back!" she exclaimed and then hugged me. "I missed you guys."

I hoped when she said guys, she meant me. I was relieved to see her. We had shared classes when I was a postulant. I thought she might have moved on while I was in the novitiate. The thought of never seeing her again had left me sad.

Mia had a contagious ease. It meant I was able to talk to her without disintegrating into a self-conscious mess. She was a couple of years younger than me. She had short brown hair that framed her face in soft brackets, welcoming eyes and full lips, an earthy voice, and an openness that was all joy and trust. She saw good everywhere and in everybody and had the charismatic inclination to give thanks and praise for it all. I might have found that grating from anyone else, but from her, it was the guileless song of her soul. And when she looked at me with those eyes, I wanted to be the good man that she saw, and I wanted her to see as deep inside me as could be seen.

"My dear friend, how have you been? How was novitiate?"

"It was pretty tough."

"A time of trial! But here you are. You made it. Tried and true."

"I guess so. How have you been?"

"Busy! Especially with prayer ministry. There's so much hardship in young people's lives. Such a need for God. Such spiritual hunger out there. I have prayed with a lot of people. They open their hearts. It's beautiful to see. Grace comes, blessings come. My goodness. But who am I to tell you? All that powerful spirituality from Saint Teresa and Saint John of the Cross."

"It sounds like you've been doing good work."

"Well it's God's grace that does the real work. I do what I can. I'm just so glad you're back. Praise God! I'm so happy."

We hugged again, and then went our separate ways. A current of delight charged through my chest and set my skin ablaze. I could have sung or jumped up and down or climbed to the top of the belltower and hollered with joy, but I contained this barely containable something as Julian mumbled that we needed to get going otherwise we'd be late for class.

CHAPTER FORTY-SIX

Everyone in the community took turns cooking in Melbourne. I cooked the evening meal once a week and occasionally prepared Sunday lunch. I had copied favourite recipes from my mother: beef and bacon casserole; gingered meat balls; a fish mornay that I later discovered was similar to a Fijian fish curry; rissoles that I squashed and serve as hamburgers; a mince dish named after my former sister-in-law. I cooked roasts for Sunday lunch, and as Sundays were considered feast days, I made chocolate pudding or golden syrup dumplings for dessert.

My simple food offered a tangible connection to the world I had left. A forkful of mornay and I was in the universe that I had occupied for the first twenty-one years of my life: the one house where I had always lived, the one solid wooden dining table where I had eaten every home meal, my mother dishing food into square ramekins on the kitchen bench, my father taking his seat at the window end of the table, my brother Shane at the opposite end. It came back to me in kaleidoscopic moments: intimate fragments and fleeting memories as I worked in the monastery kitchen and then sat down and tasted my food.

I walked to the shops to buy my ingredients. I enjoyed wandering through the supermarket and the green grocers. There was a butcher, in Box Hill Central, who featured cuts of crocodile meat in his display cabinet. I wondered how big the beast had been, how it had been caught and killed, and what the meat tasted like. It looked like fish. It probably tasted like chicken. It was the sort of topic I could have discussed with Sam. There was no end to conversations about food with him.

There was an Asian supermarket on Station Street beside the Baptist Church. It had abundant products in bottles and jars labelled in Chinese with no English subtitles. The narrow aisles were dark and some of the items looked like they had been there for years. Slabs of bean curd were submerged in plastic tubs and bags of rice were piled like a temporary wall waiting for a levee to break. The place had a musty, sweet smell and I wondered if Hong Kong or Beijing smelled that way.

There were piles of offerings, small bowls of food and incense sticks, outside newly opened businesses. Buddha could be seen on altars near the entrances to some shops, and red was the colour of good fortune everywhere. It was a cause of wonder to see how the world pressed into a city like Melbourne and how its suburban shops were portals to places I had barely begun to imagine.

At night I laid in bed and listened to the accelerating rumble and horn blast of the trains making their way to Belgrave or Lilydale or into the city. They rushed along the stretch, beside the graveyard, between Box Hill and Laburnum stations. I followed the nocturnal movement in my mind. The boom gate on Middleborough Road sounded its bell and came down; traffic stopped; the train hurtled past, groaned and screeched to a halt; people emerged from the shadows of the station to step on board; the whistle blew, the flag was waved, the motion recommenced. Light swallowed into darkness. Darkness pressed back by light.

All of this was a single thread in the great web of light that spread across the landscape: train lines crossing the flowing threads of headlight white and brake light red; the pooled light of stations; the takeaway neon along main roads; the convergence pushed skywards in the clustered patchwork bright towers of the central business district. There was consolation and beauty in those veins of city motion weaving through the quiet of the suburbs. It was possible to go somewhere else, even be someone else, in a city whose life extended far beyond the walls of the monastery.

I heard Walt Whitman and Allen Ginsberg in the beautiful clamour of the Melbourne dark. They were there as surely as the first men of Mount Carmel, the Spanish saints, the Old Testament prophets and the elusive figure of the Messiah. I took it all in and felt it stretch me, and it felt like God was in it all, and tears trailed down my cheeks because of the sheer wondrous pressure, and I knew someday there would be a breaking open and a birth, but I didn't know what would be born and it didn't matter. All I could do was surrender.

CHAPTER FORTY-SEVEN

I had grown up with a kind of composite version of you: a little from one gospel pasted alongside a piece from another, a favourite parable here, a reassuring healing scene there, all gathered into a gentle holy-card portrait. Hey presto, there you were: a wispy-bearded white man, in majestic flowing robes, devoid of any hint of a Middle Eastern origin. That was the Jesus worshipped in the suburban catholicism I experienced growing up in the 1970s. Any hint of a radical Jesus owed more to the musicals *Godspell* and *Jesus Christ Superstar* than any direct or indirect consideration of scripture.

The first Jesus I spent serious time with, as a student for the priesthood, was a hard-arsed revolutionary who cared for the cause alone. Mark's Jesus didn't have time for the cosy domestic moments that Luke's bourgeois Jesus luxuriated in. He wasn't inclined to the high-and-mighty self-proclaiming declarations that would emanate from John's triumphal Jesus. Mark's Jesus was the Messiah of an apocalyptic cult expecting the end to come within days, maybe hours. He was a man whose behaviour provoked concern among his family who thought he had lost the plot. He had become the kind of son who would spurn his mother in the name of the cause when she turned up wanting a quiet little chat. "Who is my mother, who are my brothers? All of you comrades, that's who!" There was nothing meek and mild about him. He was on a shock-and-awe deployment, a mission of discontent hammering at the status quo. That raw intent played right through to the end. The earliest versions of gospel didn't end with any consoling resurrection scene. It ended with this mad Messiah's death scream of failure and abandonment, and the ambiguity of an empty tomb. The touch of resurrection light was added in a later version.

I felt the energy of this mad snake of a Messiah. There was a strange consolation in his darkness. If this was the Jesus I had followed into religious life, the Jesus who Teresa of Avila said was my friend, then surely the dark elements of contention had a rightful place in my communion with him. Maybe following him demanded a journey up country, into the heart of darkness, into some inevitable contact with a primal energy beyond the pacifying grip of reasonableness. Maybe ultimate truth was a steady inhalation of his iconoclastic spirit hell-bent on tearing through the veils of bullshit.

Surely, I could feel it in me as my eyes poured over the words of scripture, as I sat in my room, and then took it all to prayer in the chapel. It was a brooding restlessness. It pressed me to the walls of the monastery. It seeded questions that weren't readily answered.

Every week I carried out pastoral work in an aged-care facility. I sat with an old lady who fell through the cracks of her consciousness into a world warped and tangled by dementia.

"Quiet!" she urgently whispered. "He's coming. I can hear him. We have to hide now before he comes up the stairs."

Every week she slid back into a dark space in her childhood where a predator was heard, coming through the front door of her home, stomping up the stairs. I imagined it was probably her father: a violent abuser capable of leaving wounds still unhealed after seventy or more years. She spoke to me as though I was a younger sibling swallowed in the shadow of the shared threat. The darkness was more real to her than the sun-dappled room we were sitting in, with its cosy recliner chair and hospital bed, and the smell of industrial grade disinfectant that filled the air and almost stifled the sharper smells of age. I crooned reassurances with an almost maternal murmur.

"We are in a safe place. There is no-one to trouble us here. We are here in your lovely room."

She wouldn't respond to any of that, but she would come back to the present when I started praying. She sometimes held her own reciting the Our Father. At other times, when the surface of words proved too slippery, she provided an accompanying mumble and hum. I'd take the eucharist out of its golden container, the pyx, and hold it up. In that moment, I felt close to the priest I was on the road to becoming and the situation rang true: vulnerability meeting love; a wafer-thin good shepherd communion with a higher power.

"This is the Lamb of God who takes away the sins of the world, happy are those who are called to his supper."

"Lord, I am not worthy to receive you, but only say the word and I shall be healed."

She took the host and swallowed it with a sip of water. Sometimes she would say it was lovely and I'd think of my mother, because that was the sort of simple from-the-heart thing she might say. Sometimes the old lady's face would immediately crumble back into a state of perplexity with time and space and identity dissolving faster than the host. I'd pray for her and then say my goodbyes and continue doing my rounds. She continued sitting in her chair staring into space.

I went into a lock-up section to visit another resident. He was lost in even darker coils of dementia. He told me there were horses, beautiful beasts, that he witnessed being slaughtered just outside the window where a pretty rose garden could be seen. He gave graphic details about the cutting and the butchering, but there was little emotion in his account. It was as objective as a coroner describing the steps of an autopsy and the likely cause of death.

He pointed out other patients who aimlessly wandered the halls. He sometimes yelled at them and warned me, "Watch that one. He's a devil. He's possessed."

He was forever in a world of violence. Evil lurked in the most benign spaces. I tried engaging him in some ordinary conversation, but all roads lead into the darkness. There was no escaping it. There was no turning from it. It was all around every day and would continue to be until he died.

He joined in the simple rhythm of some prayers, but I'm not sure it meant anything to him. He took communion in much the same manner that he would take his medication. Just another thing to put on the tongue and swallow down. None of it seemed to provide any respite from his personal hell.

   I drove back to the monastery. I sat in the chapel, laid my head in my folded arms, and felt my body shudder at that darkness beyond any discernible meaning. It just was. A black, enveloping thing, cracking the solid world. A heart of darkness horror. I looked at the cross with its gnarled driftwood figure. I listened to the holler of Mark's Jesus, the screaming one, the mad one, the fiery radical who died in a state of failure, the one who originally just died and that was that. Wasn't he a Messiah for a lock-up ward? Wasn't he a man who'd cause family members to lie awake at night hoping the new medication might make some difference? I tried to push my thoughts down the Carmelite road: the paradox of divine dark intimacy, a purifying embrace beyond the scope of the senses, a dark-night god's claim. The words processed through my mind with an unpalatable ease, full of themselves, as though they were sufficient when they were really nothing to an old woman's child fears and a troubled man's violent visions. I fell back to the one word that was trustworthy because it was empty rather than full. It had none of the posturing of an answer. It didn't sound with that futile clanging that desperately tries to drive away the dark. It came simple and empty as space – come. But what was it that would come? What came through Mark's Jesus and Mark's words? Not something peaceful. Not something to soothe and settle the soul. Certainly not something that was about enduring the status quo. The thing that came was a disruptive storm and a dark end.

CHAPTER FORTY-EIGHT

The priests said mass every day, in the student house chapel, after morning prayer. They took turns preaching on Sundays. Finch preached from the chair with his eyes firm shut and his face clenched as though trying to overcome a state of metaphysical constipation. He was a man whose central preoccupation concerned the undeserved and unpredictable gift of divine truth and beauty in the world.

His sermons were crowded with a great congregation of crises-ridden, morally challenged, emotionally bankrupt, neurotic characters. Some spied the lovely light of God's presence in the grimmest circumstances even in their own infidelity. Some embodied the glory of God, showed the form of Christ, within their troubled faces and hard-weathered lives. He preached that one message in which he ultimately put his hope: that saving grace is unearned and freely given and often most clearly recognised by the most broken people.

Ryan flew to more ethereal heights in his preaching. He shared whatever theological ideas he was currently engaging: a rich vein of thought from a book he was reading, the interpretative layers of a phrase about Christ in scripture, a reflection that wove together an ascetic disposition with an aesthete's sense of wonder. He gave no thought to pitching easily accessible ideas or tailoring a message in terms of any contemporary relevance. The mystery was ever relevant, and it was right to feel challenged and stretched when pondering it.

His sermons expressed that stretch of mind and heart as he tried to find right words, saying one and then discarding it in favour of another, sounding a prolonged ah ... as he reached to capture some trace of the uncapturable. It struck me, as I listened to him, that this was the sound of someone reaching towards God. There was something raw and immediate about it. It was a thing of bewildering wonder and beauty, and unlike any preaching I had ever known.

Breakfast was the same scene repeated every day except Sundays, when guests were invited to join the community. Ryan stood in the corner of the kitchen, leaning over the newspaper, with his toast and coffee at hand. He tackled food with a full-bodied, physical relish and had a habit of wiping his mouth with his forearm much like a little kid. Sam reheated whatever leftovers were in the fridge and chatted to anyone who seemed even vaguely inclined to listen. Checkers quietly ate a sensible breakfast then scurried to his room. Finch came in, gathered what he wanted, then strode to the lounge room with his mug of coffee and the other newspaper tucked under his arm. Julian stood at the toaster absorbing everything that was said, while occasionally throwing me a look to signal some significant utterance that I, more often than not, failed to register. If he heard a comment that put his nose out of joint, then he'd be in my room debriefing before class. I knew it was going to be a good day when Julian didn't need to debrief.

There were classes at the college every weekday morning. Lunch was an informal affair back at the monastery. I often ate on my own, in the dining room, and made the most of my chance to finally read the newspapers. I thought of Ivan as I read about the escalating violence in Croatia. The celebration of their impending independence in the middle of 1991 was soon lost in intensifying conflict. Ivan said he might go back after he left the order. I wondered if he was there now. I found it hard to imagine him fighting. He wasn't exactly fit or cut out for marching around in a uniform. But I could imagine him bellowing "vive l'independence, bloody!" I hoped he was OK wherever he was.

I took my seat for the morning theology class. It was March 1992. I noticed an extra degree of agitation in the air. There were whispered asides, shaking heads, arched eyebrows. It could have been due to anything: the latest bombastic utterance of the auxiliary bishop George Pell or some statement by the inquisitorial cardinal Joseph Ratzinger; something concerning the ordination of women; maybe a new development in the push to move from the one-to-one business of the confessional box towards a collective community liturgy of reconciliation. Such were the hot issues and preoccupations in the liberal theological college in the early 1990s. In retrospect it was a time of calm before the perfect storm.

The class was about to start when a woman, in the front row, turned around to face the rest of the students.

"Did anyone else see *Compass* last night?"

A few people said they had seen it. There seemed to be a murmured consensus that last night's episode of the religious affairs program delivered a significant and shocking revelation.

Julian sighed. He leaned across and whispered in my ear.

"There goes any chance of discussing theology. We're in for some TV review, no doubt followed by talking about the latest edition of *The Tablet* and that'll be it for another wasted day in this god-awful college."

"Women are being abused by clergy," the woman who first spoke continued. "It's patriarchy at its worst."

"You know what I thought?" asked another student. "Would this happen if power was shared, if women were ordained, if we had female bishops?"

"No way," replied a couple of other students.

"No! There would be transparency, accountability. But instead what have we got? Men in power behaving badly."

I hadn't watched the program, but I followed the subsequent stories and editorials in the newspapers. The religion writer in *The Australian* described the *Compass* program as full of innuendo, ill-conceived and motivated by an extreme feminist agenda. The Brisbane Anglican bishop, Peter Hollingsworth, was quick to come out with a statement that the church did not try to hush up instances of sexual misconduct. Later statements from various churches acknowledged there were instances of women being abused by church leaders, but the percentage of those incidents was far lower than the *Compass* program suggested. And yet, over March and April, there were reports that the lines of telephone counselling services had been flooded by people reporting sexual abuse after the *Compass* program had aired.

It wasn't long before the abuse coverage moved into unimaginably dark territory. I read the early reports about priests sexually abusing children as though they were terrible atrocities occurring in some distant land. The early stories, involving large groups of victims, were reported from the United States. It was awful, but I told myself it was over there; whatever the problem was it was in places like Chicago and Boston. But the stories came ever closer, like a dark creeping tide, as I sat and read the newspapers through 1992 and 1993. There were reports of Australian priests up on charges. It was in the world of people I might cross paths with one day. Maybe it included people I had already met. I hesitated before reading the local reports. There was something terrible in the proximity of the stories. There was something terrible in my moment of hesitation. I felt the beckoning delusion of safe ignorance: surely it was safer not to know. It was as though the child in me felt the threat and wanted to shut its eyes, block its ears and hide. Hide and it might pass. Tell another story loud enough, a bright and happy story where the solid world stays solid, where bumps in the night are nothing but wind, where churches and schools and camps are safe for kids, and the evil might shrink into nothing. Yet I was a man, and on the path to becoming a priest. I needed to know the truth about this clerical world I was entering, including its darkest aspects. I read the newspaper reports and recognised the evil. It wasn't over there. It was close. It was in Victoria. It was in Tasmania. It was in New South Wales. I tried to reassure myself it was the failing of individuals and not some fundamental failing of the church. Most days I almost believed it.

CHAPTER FORTY-NINE

It was Saturday morning. I was on a train rattling between Flinders Street and Spencer Street stations. I liked being alone on the train. Sunlight spilled through the windows as I read a paperback copy of Dante's *La Vita Nuova*. He was describing Beatrice, the great love of his life, who he adored from a distance. It was all very messy. Dante spent most of his time weeping and feeling overwrought by her beauty and the insurmountable sense of distance. Sometimes he came across as an obsessive stalker. Yet I understood some of those feelings he described: the joyful devastation that beauty brings; the sense of perfection that distance preserves.

I read Beatrice. I thought of Mia. I looked out the window at the passing skyline, the endless cranes that clawed the sky, the shadowy recesses of lower Spencer Street, the rattle and slide of trams, darting figures crossing the road. My mind drifted across words and sentiments that spanned seven hundred years, across the impressions of the moment, across thoughts about religion and desire. I remembered a woman speaking in a recent theology class.

"The trouble with the church is it relegates women into the role of saints or whores," she said. "Women are there to be put on a pedestal and worshipped, like Mary, or they're seen as the embodiment of temptation, like Eve. It's like one or the other, and I say neither thank you very much."

The women in the class met her statement with applause.

The train bumped and screeched around the corner. My mind drifted further back as we passed through Spencer Street Station and plunged into the underground loop. It was the mid-1970s. It was exciting going on a school excursion even if it was just a two-block walk. We were a mob of seven- or eight-year-olds, hand in hand and under the supervision of our teacher, trooping down to the local library. The library was beside the pedestrian overpass on the main road. My heart turned skittish at the sight of that overpass. Just the thought of going up the concrete stairs and taking the narrow walk over the busy main road sent my head spiralling into a vertiginous frenzy. I was glad we didn't have to climb the overpass to get to the library. I wouldn't have to stare straight ahead and not think about the cars underneath or the creaking noises that were a sure sign of imminent catastrophe. I wouldn't have to deal with the panic, the fearful crazy heartbeat, the pain of making a death-defying crossing.

I had always been prone to enthusiasms. I had a particular interest in the organs of the body at the time of the excursion: the way the heart was nestled in the midst of a great billowing pair of lungs; the way the throat lead down to the stomach; the way the stomach was full of an acid that could burn but was somehow safely contained; the way the small and large intestines twisted and filled the belly. I looked at maps of the body, in the old encyclopedias we had at home, to explore the way arteries and veins spread through every part of the body.

I plunged into the world of anatomy with great

imagination. I was inspired by one of my favourite movies, *Fantastic Voyage*. In the story scientists, in a submarine, were shrunk and injected into a body. In my imagination I was always brave. I thought it would be the most amazing thing to travel through that complex world hidden under skin and bones.

We weren't in the library for very long before my eyes caught sight of a children's anatomy book. It was the perfect book. It had great illustrations of every organ and the way they all fitted together. The other kids had the usual storybooks. I had a book about the body. I felt grown up and on the brink of some great knowledge. I took out my library membership card, went up to the librarian with a triumphant smile, and watched as she stamped it out for me. I clung to my great treasure all the way back to school and couldn't wait to take it home and show everyone.

Mum was in the kitchen slicing onions for dinner.

"We went to the library and I got this," I said as I handed her the book.

She smiled and started leafing through it, and then her face became pale and tense. She wasn't happy. She looked at me with angry eyes. I was confused.

"They let you take this out?" she asked as she pointed at a series of drawings of boys and girls showing their bodies from birth through puberty, adult life and old age.

I nodded. The next thing I knew we were in the car driving to the library. Mum was having firm words with the librarian. I was embarrassed and confused. Mum wanted the librarian to take the book back, but she wouldn't. The librarian said something about not being able to take it back on the same day it was taken out. The book returned home with us. Mum wasn't happy.

"I'm putting it here," she said as she put it under the box of man-size Kleenex tissues in the kitchen, "and you're not to look at it."

There was no way I was going to touch that book. It was obviously troubling and dangerous. It was possibly the most-evil thing on earth. I was bad and in trouble for bringing it home. Mum's reaction said it all. I had no idea what the evil was. I guessed it was something about the drawings, maybe the blood and guts inside the bodies, maybe it was the strange black hair between the adults' legs. Evil was clearly a mysterious and bewildering thing. It had something to do with bodies. I had never seen Mum so angry. I never knew I could be so guilty without even knowing why.

I was in the bathroom that night, cleaning my teeth, when Mum came in. She was angry again.

"You looked at that book again, didn't you?" she said. "I told you that you weren't to look at it, and I know you did."

I hadn't touched the book and I told her so. She accused me of lying. I was full of shame. It burnt red hot in my face and sent tears down my cheeks. I suspected my brother had heard the fuss about the book and taken a look, or that it had just been knocked out of place by someone passing. Mum was adamant I had looked at it again. She was certain of a guilt in me that was beyond my comprehension.

CHAPTER FIFTY

The boys I grew up with were getting things right and wrong in their early relationships, while I was in a monastery. They were learning the range of their own physical and emotional needs, the labyrinthine wonder and challenge of relationships, and the mysteries and practical measures that nurture genuine intimacy. They were breaking hearts and having their hearts broken, feeling the world end and reborn with every relationship, and gaining maturity with every cycle of their personal dramas. The greater portion of these experiences were beyond the walls of my monastic life with its celibate priesthood-bound trajectory.

Novitiate was over, but my sense of being subject to scrutiny and judgement continued. I could no longer associate the troubling source of these feelings with old men voting on my future behind closed doors. That business was in the past. The fatherland now lingered in the synaptic shadowland of my own mind. It took up and wove together my lifelong feelings of precariousness and self-doubt. It drew hidden nourishment from the mystifying early lessons of shame. It sought out authoritative allies from the long span of the Christian tradition. It whispered with the voice of one saint or another, wedged my spirit from my flesh, hauled my feelings into the dock for relentless cross-examination.

"Would you concede that it only takes a thin thread to prevent a bird from flying?"

The little Spanish mystic, John of the Cross,

emerged from the dark of my mind with the eloquence of a poet and a fine-tuned sensitivity in service of a divine prerogative.

"I suppose," I replied, with hesitation. I already knew where the little man was going.

"And would you further concede that a bird rendered flightless is in a sorrowful condition given its nature?"

"What does this have to do with me?" I snapped.

"It is a simple question," he patiently intoned. "Would you further concede that a bird rendered flightless is in a sorrowful condition given its nature – yes or no?"

"Yes."

"Have you taken vows committing your life to God wholly?"

"I've taken vows for twelve months," I precisely asserted.

"And is that twelve-month commitment not based on the view that this is your life calling, a calling to live wholly for God for the rest of your life?"

"Yes," I replied.

"Do you further concede, according to the knowledge you have gained and the experience of your own heart, that living wholly for God can be precarious and uncertain?"

"It isn't easy."

"And is it not made more difficult where desire is focused away from God?"

"I'm not sure."

"I put it to you that you know the truth and your feigned ignorance is itself a sign that you are on the track of self-deception. I put it to you that you are binding your heart to this girl. I put it to you that you are called to soar to a height beyond the grip of anything and everything but God alone, and you must cut even the thinnest thread that may prevent your flight."

How many threads would I have to cut in my life and what would be left of me when all my threads were cut? I understood the logic of detachment, but there was something in its application I didn't trust. Maybe my mental version of the mystic had it wrong. I knew one thing for sure. I couldn't work this out alone, so I turned to Ryan.

Our meeting started in the usual manner. We shifted piles of books to make space in his room. There were books on his bed, towers of books on his desk, and piles on the floor and the chairs. It was a world of papers waiting to be marked, journals waiting to be read, a half-written article for the Jesuit magazine *Eureka Street*, a pile of major theological works, and all manner of academic detritus. The messy room seemed at odds with the man's simple asceticism, but it fit perfectly with his prodigious intellectual appetite.

We sat in the worn recliner chairs that had been salvaged from a suburban roadside furniture dump. I tried to mirror his easy disposition, but my heart raced. I was going to tell him about my feelings for Mia and my struggle to determine if there was some appropriate place for those feelings within my religious life.

"You know Rob, I think sometime soon, you might fall in love. Maybe you already have?" I was taken aback. I was yet to say a word about my predicament. It was as though he had read my mind. There was no sense of critical judgement in his tone. I relaxed. I knew this was going to be OK. I could tell him what was in my heart.

"Yes. There is someone I have feelings for."

"Ah ..." he replied with a smile, "this was bound to happen."

"I suppose I'm left wondering about it," I said with my own Ryan-like meandering reflective tone, "I mean I'm in the monastery, I've taken vows, what does falling in love mean for what I'm doing here?"

"Well, it speaks of your humanity," he said with his head slightly tilted to the side, "You are called as this man, Rob, and all that entails. The call to Christ, and your response, concerns the whole, indeed must concern the whole: vocation realised in the fullness of your life in all its particularity."

I had spent years imbibing the man's way with words. There was something seductive in being gathered into the current of his theologising and rendered a worthy subject for his serious spiritual consideration. It was easy to become lost in his hypnotic tone, his drifting words, and the general vagaries that one might expect from an oracle.

"But I have these feelings for her. What should I do?" I asked hoping for something clear and specific.

"The grace of vocation isn't found in anything other than life as it is experienced. Grace is met in this moment, in all that is experienced here and now.

It's rightly met in and through openness to God, precisely through that experience. Ah ... now that openness is critical. It is a love concerned with the bounty of God. The recognition that this experience is indeed from the God who passes in haste as John of the Cross says; that this other is not God, but indeed from God, and leading to God, and the love the other engenders is right and appropriate within that greater movement of the heart to God. Where that openness is absent, is closed by means of a seizing upon as though this other is the end, then what occurs could rightly be considered antithetical to genuine love and, to some degree, a turning from God."

At this point he recalled an article that he had recently read that might shed further light on this matter. He dove into a wooden chest, beside his desk, to retrieve it.

"Are you familiar with the significance of Adrienne von Speyr in von Balthasar's life?"

He pulled out the article and handed it to me. The conversation drifted on for some time longer, and by the end, I could barely recall why I had gone to see him in the first place. I thanked him and left with the feeling of a dazed, but strangely elated head, that I often felt after conversations with him. I presumed, when I was a postulant, that the thick fog of his words was due to his seeing and speaking from some higher plane. As a student, I was starting to have my doubts.

I tried to construct some workable understanding

from what I had just heard. I took it that it would be OK to continue to be Mia's friend, and even allow some degree of closeness, as long as God was solidly planted in the picture. This was good. This was better than good. I had consulted the monastery's in-house expert in spiritual matters, and as far as I was concerned, he had given me a vague mystical thumbs up. God wanted me to see something of his beauty through Mia. I would look at her and surely love God all the more because of what I saw and felt. Loving Mia was part of my loving God. Simple as that.

CHAPTER FIFTY-ONE

I saw Mia in class, the next morning. We talked in the break. She mentioned she was going to be in the college prayer room that afternoon if I wanted to come for a chat. I was nervous and excited. I wasn't sure what might happen. I had Ryan's idea of openness to God, grace through experience, playing in a loop in my head just to keep me on the right track.

I went through the college, later that day, and found my way to the room. It was the kind of set-up the priests back in the monastery would have mocked. There were colourful cushions scattered over the floor, 1970's style pastel wall hangings, a couple of sticks in a pot sending up a lingering trail of incense, and a small tabernacle on a coffee table in the corner alongside a red sanctuary lamp. I could almost hear Finch suggesting the decor resembled the interior of a Bangkok bordello or Ryan throwing out one of his dry disparaging comments about people needing to have a comfy time with Jesus.

Mia was sitting against the wall. She looked up and smiled. "Oh. You came. I'm so glad Rob. Come and sit down."

I sat on a cushion beside her. We hugged.

"I haven't been in here before," I said.

"Really! I love it here. It's a peaceful place, away from everything. How are you?"

"Good," I said as I tried to settle and ignore my heart's tribal rhythm. "I hope I haven't disturbed your prayer."

"Oh no. It's fine. Maybe we can pray together?

Would you like that?"

"Yes."

"Can I?" she asked, as she placed her hand lightly on my shoulder.

"Jesus, I want to thank you for my dear friend Rob. I thank you for the blessing that he is. I thank you for his valuable witness, his beautiful vocation, his deep faith. Lord, I ask that you continue to bless him as you prepare him for his work, his prayer, the good that he will do for your kingdom. Amen."

"Amen."

Her voice gave a warm intimacy to her words. They were words for me and for God and imbued with a love and trust I could feel. I started to pray.

"Lord Jesus. I pray for my friend Mia. I thank you for the great work she is carrying out, particularly among young people in our community. I pray you send her abundant grace and inspiration, so she can continue to share your message of love and healing. I pray you might touch her heart, so she might experience the fullness of your love for her. I ask this in Jesus' name. Amen."

"Amen."

We hugged again then sat together talking about study, her ministry and my life in the monastery. Had I ever spent this much time alone with a girl who I wasn't related to? Had I ever felt such ease with a girl before? No and no. This was a foreign territory that I really liked. I liked sitting beside her, on a cushion, on the floor of the chapel. I liked her warm voice and the way she looked at me, sometimes with a heartfelt earnestness and other times breaking into a smile. I pushed aside the momentary thought that this was too right to be right. Mia. If such love was alright, then everything would be alright. I felt incandescent. She seemed happy. Did she feel what I felt? Maybe she was always like this. Maybe this was no different from the moments she shared when she ministered to countless others. Maybe this was what normal friendship felt like. I couldn't ask her what she felt. That seemed beyond the bounds of what might be appropriate.

I started to feel skittish. Too many thoughts were stealing into my mind. If I stayed I might say too much. Ruin the moment. Ruin everything. I quickly got up and said I had to go. Did she look sad? I wasn't sure. I walked back to the monastery with joy still buzzing through my body. Had I ever known this kind of happiness? Never.

Julian appeared around a corner when I walked in the back door of the monastery. "Where have you been?"

"Just out."

"Where?"

He could see my barely suppressed smile.

"What's going on?"

"I ran into Mia."

"Where?"

"The prayer room at the college."

"The prayer room. Since when do you go there?"

"Well, I ..."

"What's going on Rob?"

"She said she'd be in the prayer room and I was

welcome to drop in."

"Drop in, yeah right. What were you doing there?"

"Nothing. Well, we were praying actually."

"Rob, are you mad? What were you doing? Laying on hands was it?"

"Nothing."

"She's nothing but a camp follower, Rob. You know that. She's at the college to get herself a man. I saw it before, at the seminary."

"She's not like that."

"Well, she's clearly got her claws in you, hasn't she? You're such a fool. So clueless. You risk your vocation for what? You need a good spiritual director."

"I talked to Ryan."

"And?"

"He said I should be open to the experience."

"What?"

"He said ..."

"I don't care. He's an idiot. You're playing with fire. You're going to ruin everything. You can't see her again."

"I will."

"She's a slut, and you're throwing your vocation away."

I walked away. My heart was pounding. In the briefest space of time, I was robbed of my joy. I walked straight through the monastery, went out the front door and crossed the road. I wove through the suburb, past the cemetery entrance, the adjacent stone mason and the tattoo parlour. I crossed over the train line and briskly went past the library and the local TAFE towards the shops.

The only way I could ease the pressure in my head was by losing myself in a crowd. I needed people around me. I needed to lose myself in ordinariness. If I had stayed in the monastery and gone upstairs to my room, my rage would have spiralled, and I was afraid of what I might have done. Thrown something. Broken something. Screamed. Stormed down to his room. I could feel violence in my body. It seemed impossible to imagine that I had just been full of so much joy. A loop of torturous replays ran through my mind: the snide smirk on Julian's lips, his vile misrepresentation of Mia, the ever-so superior intonation of his voice, his relentless craven need to control.

I forced myself to breathe and focus on what was around me: a mother and her child walking hand in hand towards the train station entrance, an old lady with a pull-along shopping bag heading home from the butcher - a couple of chops and a string of sausages wrapt in plain white paper - the newsagent laughing at a customer's joke, the announcement of the arrival time for the next train.

I looked for peace in the thoughtless flow of the ordinary world. I wanted it to drive out the ugly torrent of Julian's words. I wanted to be soothed. I wanted to feel right. I wanted my joy back. I didn't want this rage. I was afraid of it. In a spasm of imagination, I saw my fist plough into Julian's face, felt his jawbone crack, his smirk shatter. Nothing but blood. An ugly end to his ugly mouth. A violent answer to his woman-hating piety. The image sparked an instinctive surge through me, a primitive knowledge in the cells of my body, in my knuckles, in my muscle fibres, the cessation of thought, an ever-accelerating torrent of punches bruising and breaking him.

But I was not that man. I had never been that man. I had never raised my fist to anybody. I had walked away from every possibility of a fight since I was a kid. Maybe that was the problem. One honest schoolyard fight might have made a world of difference. If I had fought back, then I'd have known the measure and limit of my rage. Instead there was a vacuum of experience, so my rage seemed monstrous – a crucifying force, a thing of shame and fear to be buried deep.

I kept walking until I was tired. I had robbed the rage of its energy. Now I was just sad. A sad, sorry young man trudging along a suburban Melbourne street. This was my life: a flicker of joy extinguished by a tsunami of contention.

I quietly went back to the monastery and put on my habit for evening prayer. He was there, opposite me in the chapel, with the dull weight of contrition in his eyelids. Just a touch of it. Just enough. A calculated portion to get back in my good books, while conceding as little as possible. Sorry, but it was for your own good. That sort of thing. I was glad it was prayer time. He would never bother me in prayer time. He would never cross the lines of a divinely ordained schedule. I stood and faced the front: gnarled Jesus hanging from the ceiling on his cross, the ultimate victim of everybody's rage, the cube stone altar, the peeled-back black box tabernacle. God in his box. Lucky God.

O God, come to our aid. O Lord, make haste to help us. Glory be to the Father and to the Son and to the Holy Spirit. As it was in the beginning, is now, and ever shall be, World without end. Amen. The sign of the cross, the bowing, the sitting, the back and forth of the stanzas of psalms. *Lord I am deeply afflicted. By your word give me life.* I was too tired to do anything but go through the motions. I wove the feelings of tiredness and sadness together. *Accept Lord, the homage of my lips and teach me your decrees.* I was weaving the strands and making a blanket. *Your will is my heritage forever, the joy of my heart.* I was making it thick and heavy. A shroud to completely cover me. *I set myself to carry out your will, in fullness forever.* I would pull it over myself and nothing would touch me. *Glory be to the Father and to the Son and to the Holy Spirit.* Everything inside me subdued by its weight. Everything stilled. Everything smothered. *As it was in the beginning, is now, and ever shall be.* As though I was no body at all. *World without end.* No body. No joy. No contention. No rage. No violence. Nothing. Nothing. Nothing. *Amen.*

CHAPTER FIFTY-TWO

I went about my day-to-day life as a Carmelite student, but I wasn't entirely there. I was under my shroud, quiet on the surface, quietly sinking below the surface. The change in me was so noticeable that Ryan felt the need to visit me in my room one morning after breakfast. A direct intervention like that was a rare event. Ryan was more inclined to observe from a distance. He came and stood, looking out my window, as though consulting the suburban world for the right terms of reference.

"Rob, you seem ... ah ... depressed," he finally said. It was such a clumsy observation from a man who favoured finely calibrated language.

"Just a rough patch, that's all," I replied. I needed to give him something for his effort. He seemed satisfied. He had named the thing he observed, and I had given a manageable answer.

"I don't know there's anything I can do," he said, more as an observation than a concession.

"It's OK. I'll be alright. I'll just keep going," I said.

"Endurance is certainly one of your strengths."

"Thanks," I replied, though it wasn't entirely clear he meant it as a compliment.

It was the first time I saw the man's limit. There was something awkward and discomforted about him as he continued looking out the window. This business was too personal for him. The emotion was too heavy. It couldn't be spun to some theological height. Its silence snuffed out words, and words were his reassurance. I could see that, as he stood there for a moment longer, before withdrawing back to the safety of his own solitude and his book-crowded room. And I knew for the first time that there were things about life that I instinctively understood better than he did.

His wisdom had an aeronautical intent. The great reach of thoughts and words was how he tasted transcendence. It had been beautiful to see him in those high-flying moments when I was a postulant. I had sat enthralled at his feet wanting to be like him, broken open in a space between heaven and earth. I wanted to be smart and articulate the way he was. I wanted to be that kind of spiritual man. But I could never be like him. I knew that now. And I no longer wanted to be like him.

I was beginning to feel my wisdom, if that's what the thing must be called, was bog-Irish ancient, dirt under my nails, back arched to strike, to dig and dig and dig, more instinct than thought, more emotion than words, a subterranean bid for something hidden inside mud and the entanglement of roots. The deeper the better. The earthier the truer. Somewhere down there, where my treasure was, where my heart belonged. Flesh messy and convulsive as the surge of maternal labour and the final tremor of life in a body. The thing that mattered to me had to tremble with everything otherwise it was a lie.

I might have felt hints of that wisdom, but I was depressed. A part of me that had started to come to life was now muted. I smiled and said hallo to Mia when we crossed paths between classes, but I no longer stopped to talk to her for longer. The thing that could have been was gone. I told myself it wasn't worth the grief. I sat in the chapel staring at gnarled Jesus on his cross. There it was: the never-ending cult of dying, dying to self, dying to live for God alone, dying for you.

I was disconnected from Mia, but Julian was still there. Day in and day out. There in the chapel. There at breakfast. There in the shadows of the library listening for any hint of treachery or betrayal. There beside me on yet another night walk, through the suburbs, interrogating me about things he had half heard me say or things that he had heard one of the friars say to me.

The thing is, I still considered him my friend, even my best friend, despite those moments when he snarled and snapped with religious intensity. I wasn't going to miss the bus this time. I was determined to remain his friend. If there was something of the cross about it, then surely that was appropriate given my religious circumstances. Besides, it wasn't all bleak endurance. There were still good moments. The best times were always at a distance from the monastery and the religious atmosphere that bent his nature in such an ugly way. We explored country Victoria together. We went to the football together. There were always enough genuinely happy moments for me to convince myself the friendship was weighted more to the good than the bad.

Sometimes religion reached into those ordinary moments, beyond the monastery walls, and his Jekyll-and-Hyde routine caught me by surprise. It was a cold and wet Fourth of July in 1992. Round sixteen was a critical moment in the football season. It was the weekend when finals-bound fortunes were made or lost. Hawthorn was up against Geelong at Kardinia Park in Geelong, so Julian and I were in enemy territory.

The locals were chanting for a Cat Attack and praying their born-again god, Gary Ablett, would reign supreme under the troubling grey skies of Corio Bay. The brown-and-gold contingent were hoping a solid performance by Jason Dunstall would put Ablett to shame on the scoreboard.

It was the dying days of games played at suburban grounds where people stood exposed to the elements, shoulder to shoulder, duffel coated, scarf wrapt, tribally bound, sacrificing their voice boxes to the god of war and glory. The slick, corporate version of the game, pushing national expansion and played in mega-stadiums with giant screens, was already looming. The MCG had been transformed with the Great Southern Stand. South Melbourne was long lost to Sydney. Fitzroy was soon to be subsumed into Brisbane. All things were indeed changing.

It hadn't been an easy season for the reigning premiers. I had seen the Hawks go down to St Kilda at Moorabbin and lose to Footscray at Whitten Oval. I had spent Saturdays sitting on the wooden benches in the bare shell of our windy Waverley home-ground, as my team won some and lost others.

I was standing in a crowd at the stalls in Geelong, drenched to the bone as I rocked back and forth, peering over the shoulders of the people in front, keeping track of the flight of the ball: a collision and grunt of bodies, a quick handpass, the smack of boot to leather, a spray of mud, hands out to take the ball: strong hands, chest mark, job done.

Dunstall was in top form in the forward line. He hammered in one goal after another, and when he cracked his hundred goals for the season, there was a great cheer and spectators spilled onto the ground. My team found their stride in the rain and the mud, and won the game by nineteen points.

Julian was in the driver's seat on the journey back to Melbourne. I was happy to sit in the passenger's seat and bask in the high of a victory. I wanted to stay in the moment for as long as I could.

"Hey," said Julian, "grab my breviary in the back. We might as well do evening prayer while we're driving and get it out of the way."

It wasn't an unusual request. There had been plenty of times when I did as he asked. I would read the prayers, the psalms and readings as he drove. He responded where he could. The work of prayer was then done, and the rest of the day was there to be enjoyed. But praying evening prayer was the last thing I wanted to do in that moment of ordinary joy as we drove out of Geelong.

"No, I don't feel like doing it now."

He bristled. Surely he must have misheard me. It seemed like I had just said no. He looked across at me with a slightly startled look.

"Go on. We can get it done and get on with the day."

"No. I just want to enjoy the drive."

Now he realised I was definitely saying no. He gripped the steering wheel a little tighter. His hands were white with tension. His cheeks started their bony flexing.

"Rob. Get the breviary and start evening prayer." His volume had gone up.

"I don't want to."

He took one hand off the wheel, reached back for his breviary, then threw it on my lap. "Just do it."

"No."

He slammed his foot on the accelerator and the car surged towards the back of a semitrailer.

"Read the fucking prayers," he yelled, as he swerved at the last minute into another lane to avoid ploughing into the back of the semi.

"No."

He started swerving between lanes with no thought of the other traffic. He nearly side-swiped a couple of cars. He nearly went into the back of a bus.

"Stop being so fucking stupid and read the fucking prayers," he screamed, as he continued swerving across the wet lanes of the freeway.

I took deep breaths. My heart was racing. This scenario wasn't new to me. I had spent a lot of time as a student, keeping him placated. I was cautious in my conversations in the community because, more often than not, he was somewhere listening. I studied subjects that bored me to death because he deemed them solidly catholic and appropriate. I put an end to a friendship with a girl, because he was threatened by it. A great part of my student days was spent and bent in submission to him. And the truth is, in all that, I made debilitating choices and allowed him to be the convenient conservative excuse for my not throwing myself wholeheartedly into the possibilities of a greater life. Paddy had been right in his judgement, even if his solution left a lot to be desired, back in the days of the novitiate. There was something not quite right about the tight grip of the friendship. Julian and I were both trapped in that car.

I settled into some detached space beyond the shot of adrenaline that was coursing through my veins. I calmly waited for him to kill us both. Maybe the whole journey of religious life was destined for that final moment. Two seminarians tragically killed on the Geelong freeway. No one would have a clue about the drama that lead to the accident. *Deadly tussle over prayer time. Pious rage causes collision. Catholic jihad on our streets.*

Somewhere inside me, I wondered if it would be a relief for it to end. I was worn down and depressed. I couldn't see life was going to get any better. I let go. I was ready for impact. He came close to killing us. He didn't in the end. He settled into a sullen silence and kept driving. We drove back to the monastery, and to all the world, the friendship continued, but in my heart it was never the same again.

PART FIVE

CHAPTER FIFTY-THREE

I walked up the gravel path beside old Brother Kieran and his cat. He occasionally mumbled a word to the cat, as it wound itself around and between his legs. The prayer part of the morning was over, and now the land was calling. The whole of New South Wales was in drought. It was a bad one. Water supplies were running low. Farmers were walking off the land. The paddocks around the retreat centre were covered with dust and clusters of coarse dry stubble that offered little nourishment.

Kieran was just keeping the farm going. There was no profit selling the calves. Nobody wanted to increase their stock, and there wasn't much meat on the bones for eating. The drought had to end sometime. It was just a matter of hanging in there.

Helping Kieran had become one of my daily routines since I arrived in Sydney for my pastoral year in July 1994. The year was a break from study and an opportunity to have a fuller experience of ministry before taking final, lifelong vows and ordination. It was the first time, since joining the order, that I had significant time apart from Julian. He was sent to Perth for his pastoral year. I felt I had landed in an entirely new experience of religious life. There was a sense of ease inside and outside myself that I wouldn't have imagined possible when I was a novice. I was able to talk to other friars with freedom. I could open up, laugh, even entertain the possibility of friendship in community. No one was around a corner listening, and my mind wasn't crowded with self-editing considerations of the fatherland.

The Sydney community had changed significantly. Michael and Jimmy had gone back to Ireland. Terry had gone to Perth. JV was in an aged-care facility. Australians were now taking up the leadership roles. Ryan was head of the order in Australia. Sam was prior of the Sydney community, as well as director of the retreat centre. There was a feeling of promise in the air. Maybe the time was approaching when we could finally cut the apron strings with Ireland and become a province in our own right.

Kieran and I reached the sheds. His battered old farm ute was parked there. I started hauling bales of hay onto the back of the ute. Kieran stooped and poured molasses into a bucket, then topped it up with water. His tongue poked out the side of his mouth, as he mixed his brew with a solid stick. He was an earthy, old, bull-headed alchemist at work in his territory.

The old man drove up the rough paddock track to the gate above the sheds, once we had a full load. I got out to open then close the gate after the ute. We drove along the crest of the hill and arrived at a paddock, just west of the retreat centre, and then set to work. I hauled the hay down. Kieran clipped the string so the bales fell apart in slabs. We threw them out like frisbees, so there was a broad line of feed strewn across the ground. He started sprinkling the poor-quality hay with his molasses mix, then we were back in the ute and driving to the further edges of the property where the cattle were waiting.

"C'mon," Kieran boomed, then realised he hadn't wound down his window. He mumbled an apology, as he wound it down and then boomed his call again and again.

"C'mon. C'mon."

The cattle looked up, familiar with his call, and started meandering in our general direction.

"Tsk," he said, nodding his head towards some clueless calves.

"I'll go get the silly buggers," I said.

I got out of the ute and started running in a wide arc around the calves, so I could come up behind them and coax them in the same direction as the herd. It was uneven ground. I jumped over ruts and rabbit burrows and hoped my ankles wouldn't come a cropper. There was power in my legs, and hammer blows in my heart, and there were moments when I hit my stride that felt like I was setting the world spinning under my feet.

The calves were jumpy and inclined to fan out in random directions. I eased my pace, spread my arms wide, sometimes clapped my hands, yelled and cajoled where it seemed warranted. The animals were jittery and jerky for a while longer. They eventually settled, then went galloping towards their bellowing mothers in the main herd and the molasses sprayed food that was just ahead.

I slowed down to a walk and breathed in the wide-open space of the property. This had become my favourite moment of the day. I liked being out on the farm when the morning sunlight softened the hills. I liked the ache in my shoulders from hauling and spreading hay and the quiet, pragmatic sense of brotherhood with the old man. It left me feeling distinct from the priests who rarely ventured much beyond the retreat centre. I didn't want to be a priest like that when the time came. I liked the business of dirt and callouses. I even liked the smell of cow shit that tumbled from one spooked old Bessie or another. The whole thing was good and earthy. It stood apart from the routine of the Melbourne student house. It gave me a sense of life in my body.

CHAPTER FIFTY-FOUR

I sat alone in the conference room. It was the night before I was due to give my first retreat talk. The room was the same unpolished space I experienced on my first visit to Sydney five years before. The old piano was still beside the door; the same tattered books were still spread over the bookshelf; the same antiquated wall-hanging was collecting dust to the side of the rows of chairs. There was something reassuring about the room's lack of polish. The decor didn't matter.

The thing that mattered came through the words that were spoken and received in the room. Those words were living things: incandescent, tender, confronting, overwhelming. There was grace in them. A parable had the power to break a person open with new life. A single phrase could stop a person in their tracks. A single word could be someone's touchstone to the better world. Metanoia in the speaking. Metanoia in the listening. All it needed was someone to speak the words. The sun had gone down, and it was dark. Tomorrow I would speak the words. I felt the enfolding strength of it. The better world was in me.

Sam had found his groove as a prematurely sagacious old man, and the retreat group were young adults who regularly came to listen to his insights. I met the group when they arrived earlier in the evening. They were a friendly mob and interested in me. I was only a few years older than them, and here I was a Carmelite friar and not far off my ordination. My presence naturally provoked questions. How had I experienced the call? What was it like to live in a monastery?

I had an idea as I sat in the conference room that evening. It was a little outside the box. I went to the whiteboard at the front of the room and started writing and drawing. I turned the board around when I had finished, so no one could see what I had done. The element of surprise was important. I was going to introduce a touch of unlikely fun to Carmelite teaching on the dark night of the soul and notions of spiritual purification.

I sat on the table with my legs dangling as the young adults drifted into the room the next morning. The touch of informality kept me settled and at ease. I could be sitting anywhere. Sitting on the dock of the bay. Otis Redding was more helpful than a saint at this moment. I wasn't the first friar to sit on the table before giving a talk. Ryan was an aficionado of that kind of physical informality. I smiled and greeted people as they took their seats. Sam came in and smiled at me as he sat down to the side.

"This is Brother Robert's first-ever retreat talk, and we only have one of him, so I encourage you to be gentle," Sam said.

The retreatants laughed then settled as I opened with a prayer. They were already old hands at this business. They knew the right responses.

"I want to talk about one of the central themes in Carmelite spirituality this morning. I think it's one that touches on all our experiences of the spiritual life."

I was relaxed. My voice was firm and friendly. I made eye contact and I could see their interest. This was going to be alright. I turned the whiteboard around and the group broke into smiles. An arts student, who had the long hair and easygoing disposition of a surfer, let out a laugh. There was something unexpected on the board: a cartoon. What on earth did it have to do with the serious business of Carmelite spirituality? How did this fit in with Sam's methodically earnest considerations about the spiritual life and the church?

"Here we can see a dog," I said, as I pointed to my artwork. "Personally, I think it's a pretty convincing looking dog. What do you think?"

They continued smiling.

"What do we see about this dog?"

"It has a chain around its neck," said the surfer dude.

"Yes. It has a chain around its neck, and the chain is secured to a stake in the ground. Is there anything else about the dog?" I asked.

"Is it sleeping?" asked an Indian girl.

"Yes. It's chained and it's sleeping. So how aware is the dog of its chain?"

"Well, it's asleep so it wouldn't be aware," she replied.

"That's right. The dog is asleep. It could well be dreaming that it's free. It might be dreaming that its racing across paddocks chasing rabbits or going on adventures in all sorts of scenarios. It might be dreaming it's eating a great bowl of food. In its dreams, it feels free, but is the dog actually free?"

"No," said a chorus of voices.

"No. In the real world it has this chain around its neck. Now along comes the owner," I say as I drew, "and he comes with a bowl of food, so what's going to happen?"

"The dog wakes up."

"Absolutely. The owner brings the food. The aroma drifts up the nostrils of the dog. The dog is woken by the scent of what it desires. And now what's going to happen?"

"It will get up and go to the food."

"Sure. It springs up," I do an impersonation of an eager dog, "and off it goes towards the object of its desire. The scent is a sign of what's desired, it gives a hint of it, but the dog's appetite isn't satisfied just smelling the food at a distance. It is utterly moved to go to the object of its desire. OK. So, what's going to happen?"

"It eats the food," said an earnest medical student.

"Well, no. Not exactly. There's a problem."

"The chain."

"Yes. The chain. The dog moves towards what it desires, but then hits the limit of the chain. It strains against that limit. The food is just there. Close but just out of reach."

"Poor dog."

"Yep. So, what will frustrated Fido do?"

"Bark."

"Yes, bark. Bark a lot. Bark like crazy. Bark until the owner unlocks the chain, so he can get to the food he desires. So, what does this shaggy dog story have to do with Carmelite spirituality you ask?"

I looked around. They're smiling and shrugging. This was fun. Sam looked nervous when I first turned the board around. He gradually warmed to my approach, as he recognised the direction of my reflection.

"Let's think about this story. The dog was asleep. It dreamed that it was free, but it wasn't actually free at all. There was this chain. This limitation. I wonder if we can relate to this. How might we be asleep and unaware of our chains?"

"Living a superficial life. Just living on the surface."

"Sure. Tell me more," I said.

"Well, it's easy to get caught up with parties and drinking and all of those sorts of things," said a girl who didn't seem like the party-going type. "And you tell yourself that you're free, that this is what freedom is, but a lot of the time you don't feel good. You feel like there must be more to life than this?"

"Aha," I said, "you feel there must be more to life than this. What is that feeling about? Where does it come from?"

"God."

"OK. This feeling – there must be more to life – comes like the aroma hitting sleeping Fido's nostrils. There must be more to life. So, what happens then?"

"You start searching."

"Absolutely. Searching is a prominent theme in the Carmelite imagination. Saint John of the Cross's great poem, *The Spiritual Canticle*, lays out the spiritual life in terms of the drama of a search. *Where have you hidden Beloved and left me moaning? You fled like a stag after wounding me. I went out calling you and you were gone.* It's interesting when you stop and unpack the poetic language: how it presents God. God is hidden. God flees. God is gone. Carmelite spirituality doesn't back away from the apparent experience of the absence of God. But what's the thing that actually wakens the soul to go out searching in those lines?"

"A wound."

"Yes. God wounds. *You fled like a stag after wounding me.* But what is that wound?"

No answer.

"The wound is about love. It is the wound that's experienced when there's been a touch or taste or scent of something desired. There's the touch: *ah, this is good, this is desirable, I want more, I need more. I'm opened up wanting, needing, looking for an answer – the answer – that is yet to come.* The wound is yearning, incompleteness, there must be more to life. So, tell me when you get this feeling – there must be more to life – when in your own way you experience this wound, this opening up of wanting, then where do you search?"

"Father Sam," said a girl with dark hair in the second row. Everyone laughed.

"OK, so what's that about?" I asked.

"Well, you know that the something more in life is about the spiritual life, it's about God, so you go to someone who knows about these things. You go to a priest or you go to a good retreat centre."

"Great. Where else might your searching lead?"

"The great spirituality books. The works of the saints."

"Absolutely. And what happens when you go to these people and places with your searching?"

"The more you know, the more you want to know."

"Yes. The wound deepens. All of these things are like the scent of the food to the dog. They're not the food. They're just the scent. And you want the food. The food is God. The wanting is for God. There is no complete satisfaction in anything less than God. OK, so let's get back to our dog and the chain. Do we have some experience of the chain?"

"We're imperfect. We fail," said the dark-haired girl.

"Sure. We do. We want to be with God in prayer, for example, but then we get distracted. We sit in a church and start thinking about lunch, or we fall asleep. We want to get along with others, but there are temperamental differences. We rub each other up the wrong way. And even when we manage to behave virtuously, we can have our boxing gloves on doing ten rounds with the irritating person inside our mind or heart. We can't quite reach where we are compelled to be. We can't quite be who we want to be, and we can't grasp the full answer to our wanting. Our own strength isn't enough. Our wanting is beyond our own possessive reach. So, what do we do?"

"Pray."

"Absolutely. The dog barks when it experiences its limit at the end of the chain. No matter how much energy it puts into going the distance, it can't make it. Our right response is to pray, to speak our needs to God, to be this wanting, searching, failing person and with all of that opened up to God. Prayer is that wound, that wanting, given voice."

"And then what though? I mean we pray, but what happens?" asked long hair.

"It's a bit of a mystery isn't it? We struggle with our limits. We pray. We are full of this wanting, but then what? Are our prayers answered? Often not in an obvious way. One of my favourite passages from Saint John of the Cross is about the transformation of wounds. He says a soul can be wounded in all sorts of ways: in his language *wounds of miseries and sins*. He then describes the Spirit as a cautery of love."

"As in cauterising wounds?"

"Yes. Exactly. Intense heat can be introduced to a wound to purify the wound and promote healing. It's heat, so it causes pain. It also changes the nature of the wound: *the wound not caused by fire becomes a wound caused by fire.* John says the Spirit, the cautery of love, touches those different ways that we're wounded – the regretful things we do, the limitations we experience when it comes to being generous or kind, the struggles we can have with obsessive inclinations or addictions – and those wounds become wounds of love. The touch, the transformation, registers as discomfort, frustrating limitation, being held back. But what is that discomforting touch? It's God entering that wounded space. It's one of those strange, seeming contradictions in experience that

Carmelite spirituality so often comes back to: the closeness and intimacy of God, the claim of God inside you, is felt as a growing sense of need and want for God rather than an answer that's experienced as satisfaction. It's answer wrapt within the experience of waiting for the answer. It's darkness that we read as absence, but that's in reality the darkness of an embrace. It's the aching depth of wanting that is, in reality, the possessive touch of God within."

CHAPTER FIFTY-FIVE

"Brother," Corey said, "I have heard many good things."

"Oh?" I asked.

"Oh yes," she said with a great beaming smile. "I heard you gave an amazing talk on the weekend. It blew people's minds. Even Father Sam was impressed. He was here earlier. He told me all about it. I think he was very proud."

"Thanks Corey. I'm pretty happy with it. It was my first time."

"First time of many brother. We need you here all the time not just for this pastoral year. You need to go finish your studies asap. We need a young friar up there giving talks, sharing that wonderful spirituality with people. It's a beautiful, beautiful thing. I know it. I see it. The work here is so very important. Anyway, so what did you talk about brother?"

"I talked a bit about Saint John of the Cross's poetry."

"Oh yes. I love that. It's full of such passion for God. *The Living Flame* brother, isn't it? You know, when I was a young girl I wrote poetry."

"Did you? So did I. I still do a little."

"Oh brother, can I read it? I know it will be beautiful. I would love to. No pressure, but I would love to."

"OK. I might be able to find some of my writing, but after I type this up."

I settled down at the only computer in the monastery and started typing up some notes I had made for an upcoming talk. It was 1994. The computer was good for word processing and little more.

I had taken to regularly working in the office. I enjoyed Corey's chatty presence. She was charged with a Filipino passion and regularly erupted with observations: a complaint about how grumpy Father Sam had been the other week; an account of her childhood in Manila and a quick lesson in Tugalog; a comment about the challenges of family life in suburban Australia. It wasn't easy completing work when she was around but there was a random, festive delight in her disruptions.

It had been a long time since I crossed paths with someone who really made me laugh.

I had made friends with an Egyptian Carmelite, named Buolos, who briefly visited Australia a few years before. He had been based in Kuwait and escaped across the border, dressed as a woman, when the Iraqis rolled into the country in 1990. He said the greatest challenge was his need to go to the bathroom when the border guards were taking forever to check the vehicle. There had been more than a small measure of Shakespeare's Puck in Buolos. He was a prankster who delighted in secretly dropping small objects into friars' capuches. His laughter was infectious, and he seemed to live life with a greater sense of freedom than a lot of friars. He decided, in the short time we were in community together, that I should teach him to drive.

"Rob," he said with a dramatic roll of the 'r' in my name. "Rob, you will teach me to drive. You will be the master. I will sit at your feet."

I took him out on a quiet country road where no other traffic was around.

"Look Rob!" he said, as he started gently weaving from one side of the road to the other. "I am dancing with the car! Is it not wonderful? I am dancing with the car."

I encouraged him to stay on the left, reminding him that I was indeed the master, but my direction was punctuated with laughter.

Buolos had only been in my life for a few weeks one summer. He brought unexpected joy into my life. Now Corey was bringing a similar joy. We had become good friends.

I finished my work and returned, a while later, with a few pages of poetry that I had written over the past two years. They were hardly literary masterpieces, but I figured Corey would be a kind enough reader.

"I will treasure it, brother," she said as she took the pages and put them in her bag, "I will read it tonight and bring it back tomorrow."

"No rush," I said as I left.

Corey was different the next morning. She didn't have a lot to say and there was an intensity in her eyes as though she was brooding over something. She wouldn't tell me what the problem was, so I sat down to work at the computer.

She rustled around at her desk behind me, and then I felt a wet, soft pressure on the back of my neck just under my hairline. Everything inside me jolted. I could feel Corey's lips and tongue. I could feel the heat of her breath and her teeth grazing my skin. I could smell her perfume. It was like nothing I had ever felt before.

It wasn't just that I was a virgin. I had never experienced a passionate kiss. I hadn't even experienced an awkward, adolescent kiss. I certainly had no idea what it was like to be a married woman's main course. Now I did. Her teeth and tongue sent a charge through every cell of my body. My long-forgotten balls were immediately defrosted from the catholic clerical deep freeze, and I was spinning in a state of wonder and dread. This was impossible. It couldn't be.

I could feel something primal inside me, reacting, filling me out, taking up occupancy: a brooding thing of muscle and flesh; a thing I had no idea I could be; the lion from my dream so long ago. I told myself I could not be that animal. I would not be.

I turned around. She had stepped back and was giggling at her audacity. Giggling. I could have screamed at her. What had she done? Things were finally falling into place in my life. Now there was this. I wished she hadn't done it. I wished she hadn't stopped. I had to be reasonable, but how could I manage calm, measured words when everything inside me was unravelling? How could I manage to be appropriate when every part of my body surged with the tension to inhale her perfumed breasts, devour her soft flesh with my mouth, spread her thighs and have her then and there?

"Why did you do that?" I asked. "You know you can't do that. I'm in religious life. You're married. I can never work in here again if there's any chance that will ever happen again."

"I am sorry," she said, "it's just your poems, they awoke so much in me. So much love. So much passion."

"You have to promise me it will never happen again."

"Yes, yes brother. I promise. I am sorry."

I walked out of the office with a hammering heart and an erection. What the hell was I supposed to do with that? Thank god for the generous cover of a religious habit. I could be twitching around down there till the cows came home and nobody would know any better. I walked towards the paddocks with two millennia of patriarchal programming running through my mind. All the cliché riddled elements were there: the incursive disruption of a tempting woman; a crisp bite unleashing fleshly rebelliousness against noble reason. This new tension was tortuous, and I resented it. It sent me into a frenzied catholic spiral of self-scrutiny.

I had responded to Corey appropriately, hadn't I? Yes. Definitely. I was clear and direct in rejecting what had just happened. I had said no and put down unambiguous boundaries. I was textbook perfect. But what about the drama in myself? Sure, I felt physical sexual desire, but I kept it in control, didn't I? I was in control in as much as I didn't act on the fierce charge in my body. Wasn't that the right response? Self-control. Resisting temptation. Not letting the body dictate the terms.

Now I was walking away. I was finding a place to cool down. That was good. Absolutely appropriate. That was exactly the right thing to do. A place to cool down. Somewhere I could breathe. It was just a matter of time. My body would settle. It had to. My heart would find its way back to its regular rhythm.

I would pray to you. Well, obviously, I would pray to you a lot. I would pray my arse off and not think about the mouth, the heat, the jolt, the wanting, and if I started thinking about any of those things, then I'd turn that into prayer. This wound of sexual wanting would become a wound of love for you. That was the deal, wasn't it? That's what I had so recently taught in the conference room. I would bring it all to you, and you would bring a dose of the cauterising Spirit and all would be well.

In the meantime, I needed to remind myself who I was and how far I had come. I had finally found my place in the order, in this pastoral year, after all those years of struggle. Years of persevering through panic attacks and uncertainty and the fatherland and the grimace and the judgement and the secret votes and the weird machinations of the student house and the dramas with Julian and the long months under a heavy blanket of depression. All of that should have culminated in failure, but it didn't. Surely that was grace: the absence of expected failure; the attainment of an unreachable good.

Here I was surprisingly ready made for retreat ministry and actually getting along with the community. That seemed nothing short of a miracle. I was on the brink of being somebody and making a real difference in people's lives. This wasn't the time for sexual complication. Hell, I wasn't going to let my body betray me five metres from the finishing line. I wasn't going to let the erotic shockwave from an over-excited married woman's kiss on the back of my neck ruin everything that I had been struggling for years to achieve. I had a catholic clerical destiny ahead of me and celibacy was the entry fee. It was as simple as that.

CHAPTER FIFTY-SIX

I returned to Melbourne in the middle of 1995. The issue of celibacy was the one disruptive element in my otherwise settled sense of destiny.

Old JV died before I left Sydney. He was in an open casket in the chapel before the funeral service. I had never seen a corpse before. I looked down at his body and remembered sitting beside him, in the dining room, when I first visited the retreat centre. I was so overwhelmed by that strange Irish monastic world. His laughter broke the tension. I looked at his closed eyes and remembered how they shone, on frosty novitiate mornings, when he came to teach us Carmelite spirituality. He wasn't really teaching. It was more an act of personal revelation. He allowed a glimpse of something luminous in him when he talked about Carmelite spirituality. It was expressed in the open wonder of his face as much as in his words. He invited us to look at that life, wonder at the gift it offered, and feel the joyous possibility that we were called to not only make the spiritual journey laid out by the saints but share it with others. Sometimes I sat in my novitiate room, afterwards, moved to tears.

Now I was approaching the end of my training, and I could see that I was changing. Spaces in me that had been full of anxiety, quick judgement and paranoia were filling with tenderness. I particularly felt it when I thought of the old Carmelite men. There was tenderness for JV who had shown me the power of sharing spirituality. There was tenderness for old

Kieran, the murmuring old man of the earth, as he wandered up the gravel path accompanied by his cat. And there was tenderness for Paddy. Yes, Paddy. Maybe most deeply for Paddy. The drama of institutional role-playing and all its disturbing resonances were behind us. I was able to see him clearly. I was able to see a kind, thoughtful man who often encouraged me to take care of myself.

Where did this tenderness come from? What did it mean? Was this the real business of cauterised wounds? Scoured by all manner of feelings until there was space enough inside for a cathedral of tenderness. It didn't really matter what this was about. I didn't have to understand it. It was there. It was good. And couldn't I name this tenderness brotherhood? Was there any truer name for it? Surely that's what it was.

It was all in front of me: a compelling sense of ministry; a deepening sense of brotherhood. I just had to find some appropriate way to keep my erratic sexual feelings in check.

I talked to Ryan once I was back in the student house. He smiled when I told him about the kiss on the back of my neck. He was surprisingly down-to-earth, as though I had been blooded, and we could now talk as comrades in the celibate trenches.

"Ah ... Rob," he said, "this is the first of many such experiences you're going to face. Often it will be the women you least expect."

We talked through the situation, examined my actions and intentions, and he reinforced the importance of being clear about boundaries. The conversation wasn't a great help. It framed my experience as nothing other than a battle between temptation and resistance. I could feel a deeper consideration calling, but I couldn't find my way to it, and Ryan didn't seem to be the man to help. Finch probably would have given me more down-to-earth advice, but I suspected if I went to him I would have paid for it with a torrent of his ribald asides forevermore. Julian had prompted me, over the years, to go to some local parish priests for confession. They were kind, pastoral men but they hadn't bowled me over with any great sense of helpful insight.

I suppose it was inevitable that a woman came into my life in Melbourne. At first glance, she seemed more girl than woman, peddling a lolly sweet account of her life, sketched out in an infantile manner. I could barely stomach it. It seemed a stretch to presume that you sent her to me, but there she was, so I took what she was offering.

Maybe it was her way of testing me. Maybe it was yours. I drank it down. A shock of sweet, from a surprisingly battered chalice, but then something more. She whispered me down a rabbit hole and into a dark wonderland. No lolly water now. Her soul. Her doubt. Her love in agnostic darkness. Her solidarity with the lost: those she had been given. I could feel her in my instincts, whispering into those dark spaces and memories inside me that I hadn't begun to understand. *You wanted to be a writer, didn't you? Well, I will make you a writer. Never doubt it. You can help me shake off this wretched plaster-cast form that people encase me in. Break it apart with your pen. Write down everything. Don't leave anything out. Not a skerrick. Dig and dig and dig. There's no other way to write the story of a soul. Write, and we will go where we are meant to be. You and me. Write true. Don't stop. Write for those you have been given. You will know them when it's time. This is how we budge the universe: not with a lever but a pen.*

Most people would say it was madness that I finally surrendered to lifelong celibacy based on my feelings for a nun who died one hundred years before. Maybe it was madness: a particularly catholic kind; a devotional blur of feelings and associations; a sense of her whispering presence; a murmured communion of passion and dark vision. How could I not live all my days as a priest when she inhabited my soul that way? She whispered. I wrote. I caught a glimpse of my soul in hers. I completed my final units of study, learned canon law and the practical business of hearing confessions, and I wrote a series of pamphlets for the centenary of the death of Saint Therese of Lisieux. Her pamphlets went out across Australia, landed in parishes named after the saint, some were even sent overseas. The avenues of my ministry were growing and flourishing by the minute, and I hadn't even taken final lifelong vows. How could that have been anything but a validation that I was on the right path?

I took my final vows, alongside Julian, in the Sydney chapel. Old Kieran died, in a hospital, the night before. We were both ordained deacons the following day. Family and friends gathered to celebrate. Julian bound around with a boyish excitement. I quietly gravitated to the side. Sam came and sat beside me.

"You don't seem happy the way Julian is," he observed.

I didn't know what to say. Part of me had died. I had put it to death before I'd begun to understand it. It wasn't the sort of thing to talk about at a festive occasion. Part of me had died but surely some greater part of me was about to come alive through ministry. I believed I made the right choice, the one you wanted, the one you steered me towards with my gradual feelings of belonging and brotherhood and the whispering of your saints, the one you prepared me for through all those hours when I prayed – come – but that didn't mean there wasn't grief. What is sacrifice without grief?

"I was just thinking about Kieran," I replied.

CHAPTER FIFTY-SEVEN

It was the night of 16 August 1996. The Royal Exhibition Building, in Melbourne, was illuminated and bustling with catholics. It was an unusual setting for the installation of a new catholic archbishop. The cathedral was in the middle of renovations and a sudden turnaround in church leadership had caught many by surprise.

Mild-mannered Frank Little had stepped off stage. The change was presented as due to health reasons. George Pell's appointment signalled a bombastic conservative ascendency. Right wingers were abuzz with thoughts of a leader who would unapologetically present traditional catholic positions without fear or favour. He was surely bound to make Melbourne a beachhead of conservative faith. Liberal catholics cringed in anticipation that the conservatives' dream might be fulfilled.

The exhibition space soon reverberated with old-school catholic triumphalism: a swaying procession of men in satin and frilly lace; thuribles swinging in long arcs and wafting clouds of incense to fill the dome above; a sprinkling of Latin motets; a rousing chorus of old hymns. The evening was a rowdy display of hierarchical order asserted through the power of liturgy.

The Melbourne Discalced Carmelites were in the congregation along with representatives from most religious orders and congregations in the archdiocese. Julian was on cloud nine. His hero was now in charge of the Archdiocese. The days of creative liturgies and left-leaning theology were over. Julian relished the thought that his old seminary would soon be purged of its liberal staff. There were already whispers of imminent change. Soon there would be cassocks as far as the eye could see; rosary recitations performed with military precision; conservative catholic families would come out of the cold with their endless progeny and old-school pieties. All would finally be righteously right in Melbourne.

I came out of the building once the ceremony was over, and walked towards the community van. I breathed in the cool Carlton air and was glad the whole ecclesiastical song and dance was over. Pell might be in power, but I would soon leave Melbourne. I was only three months away from my ordination to the priesthood, and then I would be back at the retreat centre in Sydney. I would get on with my prayer life and minister to ordinary people with their day-to-day concerns.

Finch was standing by the van. I could see he was agitated. I could understand his likely feelings. I suspected he felt the same as me. It had all been too much. He caught sight of me across the car park, then charged at me with vehemence in his eyes. I was bewildered. What the hell was this? He grabbed my arms and started shaking me. "Where is he? We're ready to go!" he yelled.

I pushed him away. I was outraged at the physical assault. I hadn't done anything, and I didn't have a clue where Julian was. I wasn't responsible for Julian. Finch had crossed a line. Something deep in me was triggered.

"Get your fucking hands off me!" I yelled. "Don't you ever put your fucking hands on me again! Do you hear me?"

He stepped back.

"Do you fucking hear me?"

He didn't say a word. He just blinked and stared. We were in the middle of pious crowds dispersing from Pell's installation, and I was standing there, in the brown habit of my order, ready to beat the living shit out of the bastard. I could feel my heart pounding, the surge of adrenaline, power coursing through me. I could feel rage burning in my throat and I wanted everyone to hear it. I had taken final vows, was ordained a deacon, and was three months away from being ordained a priest, and I wanted to break my so-called superior's bones. Julian then arrived. I looked at him and felt delight as his triumphal fervour dissolved into shock. Something unimaginable had happened in his absence. I had become uncontained. I had said things loudly for everyone to hear. I was beyond his control. His cheeks turned pale and drawn as he tried to calculate some solution and knew there wasn't one. We got in the van, but I was on a roll. I hadn't felt that good for years. I wasn't going to stop.

"Who the fuck do you think you are, grabbing me, you vile fucking shit."

Julian tried patting my shoulder to calm me. I flicked his hand away. His touch only caused another surge of outrage in me. His days of managing and controlling me were done. His days of clamping his hand over my mouth and telling me to shut up were most certainly over. Ryan was driving. His voice cracked and trembled as he pleaded with me to stop. Ryan tremulous and pleading. There it was. Cracks in his smooth, detached veneer. I could feel the weakness in them all. I could take them all on. Maybe I should. Maybe I would. The feeling was intoxicating.

"What was it all about?" Ryan wondered later when we sat in his cluttered room. I watched him and amused myself with a game of mental word bingo. It didn't take long at all. "Your reaction was ah ... somewhat disproportionate, Rob." Bingo. Good old disproportionate. He dissected my emotions in the same manner as he'd analyse a curry. "Is that a hint of cumin? Hmm. Possibly a little disproportionate in relation to the cloves."

Was that the spiritual life? A settled composition made of placidly reasoned proportions. Rubbish. There was a message in everything. There was a message in my rage demanding to be heard. A label like disproportionate was just another way of containing, minimising and denying. I had been grabbed. It was assault. My rage was warranted. And if there was more to the rage than the events of that moment, then it would take a journey to fully know it. I came out of Ryan's room knowing I'd rather face the storm inside me, until I knew the truth in it, than exist in the fictional world of some proportionately constructed bunker.

The final months heading towards my ordination were full of bewildering intensity. My parents came to Melbourne. Mum had battled emphysema for years. I sat with my father, in the Alfred Hospital, while surgeons broke my mother's chest open and carved off portions of her lungs, so she might have more breathing room inside. It was a last bid to extend her life. Long enough to see me ordained and hopefully a few more years beyond that.

It was life and death as I sat beside my father. The old shaming ways of the fatherland couldn't reach us in the corridors of that hospital. There was no grinning and bearing it. There was no strength to put on the regulation-issue male armour. We were fragile together looking for strength. We fingered the beads and prayed. I put my arm around his shoulders when he shook with a desolate sigh. We stared at the long stretch of linoleum and breathed in the stench of hospital disinfectant. We wondered what was going on behind the swing doors with the portholes and under the bright surgical lights. It was best not to imagine too much. Surgery is a violent business.

I was in a procession three months later. There were altar servers with incense and candles. Julian was in his role as deacon holding up the book of the Gospels. I came next followed by twenty-eight priests in flowing white vestments, and then another deacon, and finally the Archbishop of Tasmania.

My parents were already in the front row of my old parish church in Hobart. The place was full. A fair proportion were relatives. Everyone singing. *Oh breathe on me, Oh breath of God.* I was about to become the first Tasmanian Carmelite priest.

"God's holy people, that's who we are, that's what

we are," preached the Archbishop, "the holy people of God. And every serious Christian being told that, thinks something like, 'except me'." He went on to preach that thing catholics believe – God brings holiness in and through a community of sinners and the ministry of unworthy sinful men. The drama of grace in and through a church with its roles and structures and liturgies. God's work spelled out institutionally. I laid prostrate on the ground as a long litany to the saints was sung. The Archbishop placed his hands on my head and silently prayed. The deed was done. I was a priest. I had received the identity and role for the rest of my life.

PART SIX

CHAPTER FIFTY-EIGHT

The community gathered in the conference room in Sydney to meet a visiting bishop. He had been involved in the creation of the Towards Healing Process which was implemented in the same month that I was ordained. It was the church's attempt at a considered and structured response to the increasingly prominent issue of child sex abuse by priests and religious. George Pell had struck out on his own and implemented an alternative process in Melbourne.

The bishop was a matter-of-fact man. He had sat with the victims of abuse. He had heard their stories and taken them to heart. Now he sat with us and presented the most up-to-date psychological understanding of paedophilia. The friars sat and quietly listened. I told myself this was good. The church had been slow to respond, but now it was doing something positive. Surely now victims would be heard, respected, supported and compensated. Surely now the church would be the just and healing presence that it was meant to be. I needed the church to get this right. Others needed it even more. I had come a long way since I struggled to read those first stories about the sexual abuse of children in the newspapers.

Conversation opened up once the bishop finished his presentation. Someone mentioned a local priest in the diocese, who was up on charges for the sexual abuse of minors.

"Oh, the poor man!" exclaimed one of the old friars, "all the good he's done over a lifetime of ministry, not to mention his great devotion to the Legion of Mary, and this is the thing he will be forever remembered for!"

Another old friar murmured agreement, then drew breath and spoke up. "Well, you see, it's the local press. *The Illawarra Mercury* very clearly has an anti-clerical agenda. They can sniff the opportunity of attacking the church, so they're at it. All guns blazing, as they say."

A relatively younger Irish friar felt moved to contribute his thoughts. "Sure, it's a terrible thing. The abuse I mean. Terrible. But well, in a twisted way, it is a kind of love, isn't it?"

Child rape. The abuse of power. A kind of love! I couldn't comprehend the reaction of these men. I lived with them. I knew there was good in them. They weren't evil men. But what was this? Sure, they might reason their sensibility as loving the sinner while hating the sin. The mandatory *let he who is without sin cast the first stone* would undoubtedly be trotted out along with a humble reference to the immeasurable breadth of your forgiveness. But what was this first movement in these men, this first instinct of outrage and desperate rationalising, that went to the side of the accused paedophile rather than the child? Where was the spontaneous outrage, the gut-deep bellow and banshee cry, the blazing fire, the storm front of unyielding defence, for the poor raped child, wounded for a lifetime? Where was the arm raised high, taut and resolute, to drive away those who were immeasurably worse than money lenders? Where was the defence of innocence? How deep did the roots of this toxic culture spread? And what about me, there in the room, newly ordained and sitting beside them? Had ordination made me complicit in this toxic sense of clerical brotherhood? And what about my ministry? If I ministered well, promoted the church and encouraged people to enter more deeply into its life, then what did that amount to? Good cheese in a toxic trap?

I didn't have the words. Not then. I could feel something inside me. It was tectonic deep. I felt it grind. Something ancient, dark and fractured. Maybe beyond even you. Better that it was beyond you. If you could reach into that dark, then why didn't you? But maybe you are the grind within my soul. Maybe. Those friars spoke their stupid words, and my soul sounded its grinding subterranean knowledge. There in the dark. There on the edge of insidious things. There in the honesty of the senses. The place where boyhood brotherhood is made: the kind that leaves religious brotherhood for dead.

Nick was my oldest mate at school. I had known him since I was four years old. He was the complete opposite of me. He was the toughest boy I knew. He wasn't afraid to break rules and he didn't seem to be afraid of the Crying Room. We weren't allowed to go into shops after school, but Nick was so self-possessed he walked into the J Harris Fish Shop, straight after school, and bought hot chips as though it was no big deal. I once went in with him. He offered me some of his chips. It was a kind of rule-breaking communion and the chips tasted sacrilegiously good. I was shit scared, for days afterwards, that my name would be called out in the morning assembly.

There was a school camp. We stayed in bunk houses. We were raucous for a while, but settled after the adults yelled at us one too many times. Some boys fell asleep. It was dark and late. Nick was in the bed next to mine. We were quiet, and then the door opened. A teacher came in. He was everyone's favourite: a sporty, laid-back, old boy of the school. But he was more than that. He was famous. He was an international test cricket umpire and knew all the players: Lillee, Thompson, Hughes. He was the type of success the old boys' brigade near worshipped. He was a big deal, a big man, with a pocket full of jellybaby lollies to dish out to the young boys who idolised him. Everything about him said he was friendly, approachable, trustworthy. He was one of the few teachers I was inclined to trust.

I stayed still and pretended to be asleep, but watched the teacher through my squinting eyes. He went to Nick's bed, whispered something and then took him outside. It seemed like a strange thing to happen. Why would a teacher take a kid outside in the middle of the night, when we were all meant to be asleep? I laid there wondering about it, and eventually the teacher brought my mate back.

Nick started sobbing once the teacher left. It was a quiet dreadful sound, and it made no sense. Nick could cop a belting without batting an eyelid. He could talk back to the most menacing teacher as though there was nothing to fear at all. He was as tough as nails. and yet there he was spilling over with some strange sadness. I asked him, "What's the matter?" He said, "Shut up and go to sleep or you'll be next."

I shared a tent with another mate, Max, on another school camp. He had a tape that his older brother had lent him. It was wicked and sinful and wrong. It was radical and wild and right. He took it out, on the first night, fast forwarded to the second track and pressed play. We lent in to the speaker and our ears exploded with the sound of *Never Mind The Bollocks*. Just listening to it was sure to send us to hell. But in that brief moment of my twelve-year-old existence, I didn't give a shit. Rage was real and had a sound. It jerked and convulsed. It swore at the world. It banged. It screamed. It smashed at the shiny surface of things. It smashed at the holy surface of things. It tore the night with a disproportionate fury. We were just kids sitting in a tent on a school camp, but the sound of that rage rang true.

CHAPTER FIFTY-NINE

I gathered myself to you every day, when I sat with the community praying the psalms, and as I sat in private prayer in the chapel. There was still something there: the bountiful good that once shone in JV's eyes; the narrative power I had heard in Jimmy's voice; the day-to-day good that I still glimpsed in the friars around me. I trusted your deep presence abided, even underneath the ugly layers, just like Teresa said.

I dug deeper. I read the old stories. I listened for the whispering of the saints. Spanish Teresa with her pen in hand putting luminous words on the page in the Inquisitorial dark – the many rooms; the castle soul; the king who reigns in the centre. French Therese sinking into her dark gained sense of destiny – sister to an agnostic new century that was now drawing to an end; sister to my own dark travelling soul. They were still there. I could hear them. I sometimes felt they came to inhabit me. I stood in the conference room and felt them speaking through me from one retreat to another. They had a message. I could deliver it. I saw their words bring insight and hope to retreatants.

I continued looking at you. I looked at you in the hope I would discover how I should be. Ordination changed the way I saw you. Now you were a Messiah unafraid of domestic ordinariness: solving a grog shortage at a party, visiting people's homes, breaking bread with them, listening and telling stories, chatting with one girl then telling her busy sister to get over her sense of domestic martyrdom. A man who could take off into the desert but who was also at ease with others. Not just available for them but thirsting for their company. I looked at you and saw a man in the world, and I wanted to be there too.

How many of those perplexing kingdom stories tumbled out of you after one too many wines? You know the ones I mean. The parables that are never as simple as people think. How often were they first greeted with laughter, protests about their implied absurdity, playful debates about their meaning. Who the hell would leave ninety-nine sheep to find one? What's that about? The vulnerability of the many for the security of the few? Best not overplay that story these days, sunshine.

I had spent years gravitating to solitude. It had always been a mixed reality. Sometimes it was little more than avoidance of an overwhelming world: that fringe-dwelling kid in the university refectory looking across the room at the vivacious social world of others. Sometimes the solitude was all about the gravity of pondering and searching for you: that same kid, creating and searching, with his nocturnal poems and his typewriter and his afternoon visits to empty churches.

Now I felt a social gravity. Maybe it was my hunger for an ordinary life. I suspected you were in that gravity too. *In persona Christi.* You breaking me open to the wider world of other people, seeing the good in them – encouraging, delighting, learning. I realised the better world was a social business. I had spent so long believing I would find it through prayer and thinking. It was a revelation to understand that moments of the better world were waiting to be found in a friendly exchange, a shared idea, the disarming intimacy of a real friendship.

"Ah, Father Robert, how good to see you!"

Maria was a warm-hearted Samoan woman with a passion for community. "Good to see you too Maria. How's life?"

"Well, now Father, it's funny you should ask," she said with a chuckle. "You know I told you about my community venture."

"Yes, it's exciting," I said fully aware that this was going somewhere.

"Yes, it is! So, I have to give a presentation about my idea, and it would mean a lot if you could come. You wouldn't have to say anything or do anything. Just being there would be great."

"Of course. Unless I have any previous commitments. If I can be there, I would be honoured to be there. Thanks for asking me."

Of course, I went to her presentation. I didn't absorb all the details of her business plan, but I enjoyed her enthusiasm. She was all about making a difference for the young people in her community. She seemed pleased that I was there. I felt good. Priesthood wasn't just about saying masses and hearing confessions. It was about being there for people in the significant moments of their lives.

I felt good as I drove back to the monastery. I wound down the window and felt the fresh air brush my face. I turned up the radio and started singing.

Sure, there was a lot that was wrong in the church, but there was good too. This moment was a good moment. I had a part to play in bringing the better world. I turned up the retreat centre driveway, parked, then bounded up the stairs and went through to my room. I was taking some things out of my backpack when an old Irish friar appeared at my door.

"Robert, there you are. We've been looking for you. Where have you been?"

The concern seemed out of place. Ministry meant we were all coming and going, and in the days before widespread mobile phones, there wasn't any system of keeping track who was where.

"I was just at a community event," I replied.

"Oh," he said, "it's just I have to tell you something."

He had an odd, crooked smile. I hadn't lived with him for very long, and I hadn't quite got a handle on him. He was at the slightly perplexing end of the Irish spectrum. It wasn't easy to know whether he was heading towards a joke or a serious point.

"What is it?" I asked, thinking there was some amusing anecdote ahead.

"It's just there's been an accident, Robert," he paused. "It's Ryan and Paddy. They're dead. They were on their way up from Melbourne, as you know."

I stared at him. What he said didn't make any sense. Ryan and Paddy weren't dead. They would be arriving soon. We were about to celebrate the fiftieth anniversary of the friars' first arrival in Australia. I had helped put up the decorations in the larger dining room. I frowned. My mind was fading. I couldn't feel anything. I wanted to feel something. I walked up the hall to the friars' recreation room and poured whisky into a tumbler. I downed it in one gulp. It burnt a trail down my throat, but after that there was nothing. I poured again. Drank again. Still nothing. I stared out the window for a while, and then I remembered Julian was in England. He had been sent to the order's retreat centre in Oxford after he was ordained. He had to be told. He would expect me to call him. I rang. I gave the news. I cried. He cried. I was told later I had done the wrong thing. It wasn't my place to communicate the news overseas. It was a job for Sam, who was now the acting regional vicar. I nodded my head. I said something appropriate. Maybe apologised. None of it mattered. It was all just noise.

It became real when the casketed bodies arrived. They were placed before the altar, in the retreat centre chapel, the night before the funeral. I stood beside them for a while. Paddy had come to live in Melbourne in my last year there. That's when I saw him for who he really was – a kind, gentle man. I thought back to the novitiate as I stood beside his coffin.

"You know Rab, a married life is a good thing. It's a holy thing. In some ways holier than this life."

All I heard, as a novice, was an old man pitching an argument in the hope he might get rid of me. I hadn't seen him truly, so I couldn't hear him truly. But now I could hear him. I placed my hand on the coffin. Tears rolled down my face. Paddy was gone, but I could almost hear him whispering. *Life is so short Rabbie Boy. Life is so short.* It seeped inside me. It lingered in the cracks between my nature and intentions. It stayed in me as I saw the men buried in the plot of land between the chapel and novitiate. It stayed in me when I was told I was now the director of the retreat centre.

Eight years had passed since I felt the pummelling waves of Jimmy's extraordinary retreat talk. Seven years had passed since I was a paranoid novice tossed around in a world of insecurities. Little more than eighteen months had passed since Ryan and Paddy had watched the archbishop ordain me in Hobart. Now they were dead. Sam was regional vicar. I was in Jimmy's old role as director of the retreat centre. Life is short. Life is fast. It flees and then it's gone.

CHAPTER SIXTY

You know how it went after that. I put my foot down on the accelerator. Every day was busy. There was the retreat centre to run; weekend retreats and week-long retreats to preach; visitors needing spiritual direction; acommodation and staff issues to resolve; guest speakers to organise. There was a new catholic chaplaincy to set up and run at Wollongong University. There were communities of Carmelite nuns needing retreats: Lismore, Ormiston, Auckland, Launceston. And there was the everyday priest work: occasional parish masses, confessions, morning masses for other religious communities, regular masses at Saint Greg's boarding school.

The accelerating activity culminated in my first extended overseas trip at the end of 1998. I gave a keynote speech at a Carmelite conference in Taiwan followed by a retreat for lay Carmelites in Hong Kong, a bewildering period visiting Carmelites and getting food poisoning in the Phillipines, a quick visit to a community in Singapore, and then a brief stop in Sydney before flying to Papua New Guinea to give a week-long retreat to Carmelite nuns in Bomana.

I entered 1999 in an elated, punch-drunk state. The harvest is great, but the workers are few. Did I really trot out that old Matthean chestnut? You know I did. I felt a particular pride that came in weathering the overwhelming intensity of service. I had no doubt this was now my life. My limits would be buffeted by your generosity. My nature would be stretched by your grace. I had no idea that I had already entered my end times, and the whole thing would be over within six months.

Everywhere I looked there was need. It was in the searching gazes of retreatants sitting in the conference room as I spoke. It was in the vulnerable pondering of people in the confessional. I felt the need and then the responding flow: compassion, tenderness, words that heal, stories that illuminate. Surely ministry was surrender to that flow. What more could I want from life than this? I was in the flow. I was given over to it. I could feel the presence of those whispering saints and the old stories so strongly that they started breaking me open when I preached.

I became more breakable as life became busier and more intense. Maybe the line between grace and exhaustion blurred, but burnout was the language of people who didn't understand. If religious life had taught me anything, it was that spiritual destiny was a grinding thing. Ground like wheat. Isn't that how it goes? Was I addicted to that punch-drunk feeling in the end? It's possible. It felt like it was shaping me to you. Breaking me down so I became less, and you became more. I prayed –*come* – and more requests came to me. I prayed – *come* – and I saw more need for you. I prayed –*come* – and I broke a little more.

On one retreat I unpacked the original cultural implications of the prodigal son story. I reached the point where the father suddenly ran to meet his wayward son who was coming up the road. Nothing so shameful as an old man running. He was the unconstrained antithesis of the shame-filled, stifling fatherland. He was you. More than every lesson from every moment from the whole of all our lives. He was you. Spoken into presence. The great groundswell of compassionate wisdom pushing to answer everyone broken and in need. He was you as we need you. You as you promised to be. The good that breaks through everything that binds us.

Tears rolled down my face as the story flowed off my tongue as the old man ran down the road as the neighbours looked on with disdain as the calculating son watched the overwhelming force of a raggedy old man race towards him with nothing but love in his eyes. Tears rolled down the faces of retreatants. The story was alive. It took hold of the room. I felt it there as I had when Jimmy preached all those years ago. I had reached a place that I had barely dreamed I might reach. It had taken nine years, but I was there.

I was travelling towards my destiny and I couldn't get there fast enough. I planted my foot right down on the accelerator. Light through the cracks of a fast-breaking vessel. The more cracks, the more light. Shredding speed. My nothing to your all. My days were busy, and my prayer took on a heroin strike of apocalyptic urgency. All those years eating flesh and drinking blood and now the lion was in my prayer, looking for someone to eat. I directed his attention to you. I prayed – *come*. He roared – *come*. Everything in me merged into one: an arrow fast flying through a cloud: my heart, my mind, my desire, my flesh and blood.

CHAPTER SIXTY-ONE

The soothing and precocious rhythms of Grieg's *Lyric Pieces* became my night-time soundtrack during the final months in the monastery. Sam had suggested a few years before that I might like the northern European composers. He thought that their musical spaciousness, informed by fjords and wide mountainous vistas, might resonate with my Tasmanian soul. He was right. 'The Elves' Dance', 'Folk Song' and 'Cradle Song' held me with cool tenderness and unbuttoned my racing mind. Grieg helped me find my way to sleep most nights.

I had always relished my days off. As a student, it had been about getting into the distracting liveliness of the city or going to a game of football. I was drawn to anything that could get me out of my head. Once a priest, my time off was increasingly spent with a friend outside the order. She was an older woman. She loved me. I loved her. It was an innocent love that involved shared pleasures in ordinary things: frequent trips to the cinema and meals in her home.

There were moments when I felt an ache of tenderness. In another life, the ache might have found expression in a casual embrace and a lingering kiss – the natural flow of the body declaring the feelings of the heart. I just felt the ache, as she chopped onions and I poured wine, as I stopped the car outside her house after a movie and she said goodnight. I was glad the ache was there. I never acted on it. I didn't want to ruin the friendship with a moment of complicating physical intimacy. I simply enjoyed that time with my friend and my ordinary self. Then I packed that part of me away as I drove back to the monastery.

I told myself I had found some kind of balance. I had read whatever books and articles I could find about the celibate life and the need for intimacy. I knew some priests had trouble acknowledging their most rudimentary feelings. It took nothing for them to end up tied in knots of embarrassment at even the vaguest intimation of human closeness. I didn't want to be like that. I didn't want to end up some awkward stand-offish cleric. I didn't want to be afraid of my own body. I didn't believe you wanted me to be like that. I knew you weren't like that.

I sat in confessionals and heard peoples' stories. I felt awe witnessing them digging deep to name the tangled truths and falsehoods of their lives. I witnessed tears and expressions of deep regret. I heard soul-searching questions and lifelong frustrations. All I could do was channel your compassion, encourage them to listen to your voice in their conscience and in their nature, and follow your promptings, even if it led somewhere other than the officially sanctioned direction that the church taught.

Those born gay had as much right to intimate love as anyone else. Those trapped in brutal and abusive marriages were right to escape and marry again if the opportunity arrived. I came to see religion as sometimes a friend and sometimes an enemy of your better world. There were times when I came out of the confessional and wanted to scream at the church to get out of the way of peoples' lives and their emerging truths.

Then I thought about the worst things: the child abuse, the cover-ups, my own strange journey through my training to become a priest. What an ugly dysfunctional mess it all was. And when I thought of you, the truth of you, the force of you, all I preached and felt subject to, my love beyond the measure of my heart, all I could see was liberation and it wasn't enough for me to preach it to others. I could feel the day fast approaching when I would have to live it too.

A woman arrived at the retreat centre one evening. She needed a place where she could get away and do her university work. It wasn't the usual reason for staying at the retreat centre, but the place was empty, and I believed in hospitality. I fixed a plate of food for her and sat with her as she ate. She was a talker. She talked about her studies, her challenging lecturers, her favourite TV show, the miraculous properties of something called a bath bomb, and the office politics in her part-time job. My brain hurt listening to her, yet I could have sat there all night. I crossed paths with her a few more times, and we talked some more. She was friendly and just being herself, but she happened to arrive at the moment when all the forces of my life were converging.

I believed I was in love. It was as though I stepped through river mist, one winter morning, and found myself standing on the frosty grass at an old familiar bus stop. I was standing before a boy who was barely into his twenties. His eyes were directed self-consciously down. I could see the tension in him as he waited in hope that the girl across the road might come and catch the bus. I could see the troubling shadows of doubt fall across his face because he had gone through too many mornings of silent failure. He was an awkward boy on the edge of a world that seemed too much for him.

All I could do, as I stood before him, was cup his face with my hands and draw his startled eyes to mine. And when I spoke, it was with a calm authority.

"This is what we are going to do this morning," I said to him. "I'm going to give up everything, and you're going to tell that girl what's in your heart."

And the boy panicked because he saw the traces of a long journey in my face, and he was doubly afraid. I had been somewhere and become someone more than he could begin to imagine. How could this be right? How could this be true?

So he said, "But you can't."

And I said, "Yes I can. This is what we do. This is who we are."

And I held him secure, just the way you taught me, as the whole world crumbled under our feet and we began to fall through the air and into the primal waters and down into the belly of the beast.

ACKNOWLEDGEMENTS

The act of writing is a solitary endeavour but it takes a community to bring a book into the world. I want to thank the small group of first readers who encouraged me as I wrote short pieces reflecting on moments from my past. I am most grateful for the love and support of my beautiful wife Liz. She discovered early in the process that my occasionally tear stained face, at the end of a writing day, was evidence that my day had actually gone well. I want to thank my brothers, Rick and Shane, and my sister Susanne for their encouragement.

I am grateful that I was accompanied, in those early days of writing, by one of my former brothers in religious life, Greg Burke. He thanked me for sharing my memoir with him. Naming my work as a memoir helped me see that I was, in fact, on the road to something more than simply writing short pieces about my life. I was indeed writing a memoir. I am grateful for Kathryn Heyman's advice that I might benefit from aiming to show not tell through my writing. It was advice that shifted the book from an abstract reflection into something more immediate and real.

I thank those many people – all fine patrons of the arts - who generously supported me, through my Pozible campaign, in covering publication costs. Many thanks to Heather Millar for her fine-tooth-comb editing and the brilliant cover design work of Emilie van Os-Schmitt. I finally thank you reader for taking the time to journey with me through that dark wondrous period of my life. I wish you every blessing and good fortune.

ABOUT THE AUTHOR

Rob Donnelly was a member of the catholic religious order, the Discalced Carmelites, from 1990 until 1999. He has gone on to work in a number of roles in both the community and academic sectors. He has worked as a script writer and a writing mentor and is a published poet.

www.ingramcontent.com/pod-product-compliance
Lightning Source LLC
Chambersburg PA
CBHW051934290426
44110CB00015B/1974